"Inspiring and demystifying, this volume offers powerful and practical advice to all embarking on the journey that is the college search. If you decide you want to buy only one college guide, this would be an excellent choice!"
—MARK J. HATCH, VICE PRESIDENT FOR ENROLLMENT,
COLORADO COLLEGE

"At last, an engaging and entertaining student-centered college guide. Only Lynda and Eric can draw the relationship between the dating game and the college admission game and in doing so, empower students to find colleges which are a great match for themselves. From debunking myths such as the all-knowledgeable and 'scientific' *U.S. News & World Report* college issue to educating the reader with more reliable advice and tools such as the National Survey of Student Engagement, this is a great guide which will inform and entertain you. If that doesn't work, you can use it to help you find the right mate."
—BEVERLY MORSE, ASSOCIATE DEAN OF ADMISSIONS,
KENYON COLLEGE

"Finally, a guide book that speaks in the language of a college-bound student! A fun, refreshing approach that humanizes the admission process."
—JARED CASH, ASSISTANT DEAN OF ADMISSIONS,
BATES COLLEGE

"This is a great book that discusses many of the confusing, conflicting, and sometimes intimidating questions associated with the search for that perfect college match. Yet the authors address those matters in a way that avoids all of the preachy arrogance that I have found in so many other books that have attempted to address the same topic. Because the authors have such a wealth of experience with so many applicants and their families, they do not need to resort to ill-informed preaching. Instead, they often support their observations and suggestions with the strong examples that only very experienced counselors can provide."
—GARY L. ROSS, VICE PRESIDENT, DEAN OF ADMISSION,
COLGATE UNIVERSITY

# How to Be Irresistible to Colleges

## The Essential Guide to Being Accepted

Eric Dawson and Lynda Herring

*How to Be Irresistible to Colleges: The Essential Guide to Being Accepted*
By Eric Dawson and Lynda Herring

Published by SuperCollege, LLC
3286 Oak Court
Belmont, CA 94002
www.supercollege.com

Credits: Cover: TLC Graphics, www.TLCGraphics.com. Design: Monica Thomas
Layout: The Roberts Group, www.editorialservice.com

Trademarks: All brand names, product names and services used in this book are trademarks, registered trademarks or tradenames of their respective holders. SuperCollege is not associated with any college, university, product or vendor.

Disclaimers: The author and publisher have used their best efforts in preparing this book. It is sold with the understanding that the author and publisher are not rendering legal or other professional advice. The author and publisher cannot be held responsible for any loss incurred as a result of specific decisions made by the reader. The author and publisher make no representations or warranties with respect to the accuracy or completeness of the contents of the book and specifically disclaim any implied warranties or merchantability or fitness for a particular purpose. The accuracy and completeness of the information provided herein and the opinions stated herein are not guaranteed or warranted to produce any particular results. The author and publisher specifically disclaim any responsibility for any liability, loss or risk, personal or otherwise, which is incurred as a consequence, directly or indirectly, from the use and application of any of the contents of this book.

ISBN13: 9781932662320

Manufactured in the United States of America
10 9 8 7 6 5 4 3 2 1

Library of Congress Cataloging-in-Publication Data

Dawson, Eric S. (Eric Shane), 1970-

  How to be irresistible to colleges : the essential guide to being accepted / by Eric Dawson and Lynda Herring.

    v. cm.

  Contents: Prologue -- How this book is different -- The glamour of falling in love -- A few thoughts about the hype -- So? who are you, anyway? -- The importance of knowing yourself with ten questions to help -- Timing is everything -- The calendar -- Checking out the field -- Knowing your resources -- Setting up your little black book -- Creating a balanced list of good matches -- Pre-date primping -- Course work, standardized tests, and EA/ED -- The first date -- The interview and visits -- Meet the parents -- How to let your parents have a say without their dominating your every waking thought -- The love letter -- The application, essay, and other paperwork -- How to play the game -- Diversity, athletics, legacy, first-generation college, development office candidacy? -- Paying for dinner -- Financial aid, scholarships -- The wait -- Waiting for an answer -- Mixed messages? The wait list -- What can be done -- Dealing with the hurt -- Rejection -- Taking a break or "finding yourself" -- The gap year -- Love the one you're with -- Making your choice and liking it -- Marriage -- How to succeed in college: tips from former students -- When divorce is necessary -- The transfer -- Our random list of 76 colleges we like.

  ISBN 978-1-932662-32-0 (alk. paper)

  1. College choice--United States. 2. Universities and colleges--United States--Admission. 3. Universities and colleges--United States--Entrance requirements. I. Herring, Lynda. II. Title.

LB2351.2.D29 2009

378.1'61--dc22

                              2008035860

# CONTENTS

# A NOTE ABOUT TERMINOLOGY:

The authors learned all about the college application process while working at Kent Denver School. In the reading of this book, it might help you to know that Kent Denver has a very unusual college counseling program. Basically, at any given time, there are ten or eleven college counselors, making the ratio of counselor to senior about 1:10.

The counselors, all of whom are teachers, actually work as a committee, meeting twice a week to share ideas and expertise about colleges, the application process, letters of recommendation, and the students themselves. Each counselor has his or her own group of advisees, but we say, and we really mean it, that every senior advisor advises all seniors.

So, just to be clear, when we use the word "student," we also mean "advisee," and vice-versa. Likewise, if we say "counselor," we also mean "advisor" and even "teacher."

You probably would have figured that out anyway, but just in case . . .

*Dedicated to teachers and college counselors all over,*
*but especially our friends and colleagues at Kent Denver*

ERIC DAWSON      LYNDA HERRING      SAM AYRES

Hi, I'm Lynda.

And I'm Eric.

We're the college counselors who wrote this book, and, with nearly three decades of combined experience, we have a few stories to share, both about college admission and—whether you want it or not—dating. We wrote this book because while there are a lot of college how-to's on the market—too many, really—we discovered the need for one that would provide essential information for applying while calming things down a little. A number of books out there try to act like they have some sort of secret, so we want to share a secret with you: they don't. With a little guidance from us—and a few chuckles along the way—we hope to teach you what you need to know about college admission as well as a little about yourself, too (which is, after all, the first step in finding that match, both in college and dating . . .). So sit back, relax, and see where we take you.

**ERIC:** By the way, as far as dating goes, I enjoyed being single until I met my match (in more ways than one) in my mid-thirties.

**LYNDA:** And if you want to know about my dating past, it's even more straightforward: I fell in love during my first year in college, married soon after, and never once looked back. Statistically, we shouldn't still be together since we married so young. Clearly, we're here to remind people that statistics often lie.

**SAM:** By the way, in case you're curious, I'm Sam, the cartoonist. I somehow managed to survive being a student of both Lynda and Eric (Lynda was my college counselor, too). I'm at Yale right now, and I'm lucky that it's been a great fit for me (I get to do cartoons for our daily newspaper), but the point isn't that everyone has to or should go to Yale; this process really is all about finding a place where you'll be happy. While I love being a student here, it isn't the right place for everyone. So read what Lynda and Eric have to say—it'll help to find schools that will be the best fit for you—or, if you feel yourself dozing off, just look at the cartoons, and your parents will at least think you're being productive. As for my own dating life, I'll leave that to your imagination.

# How This Book Is Different

*"Love is a kind of warfare."*

—OVID

There's a reason you picked up this book. Maybe the title caught your eye. Or maybe you thought it was about dating, and, so overwhelmed by the passionless ennui of your existence, thought, "couldn't hurt." Or maybe you're one of those thorough types whose goal is to track down every college advice book ever published. Or . . . who knows? It's even possible your well-intentioned aunt bought it for you and is smiling approvingly at you this very moment.

Whatever the reasons for holding this book at this particular juncture in space and time, if you actually are starting the college search, you have all the information you need in your hands already.

Before getting any farther along, however, there's probably something you want to know—namely, what makes this book different from all the rest? It's a fair question, so here are a few answers:

1) **We cut to the chase.** Notice how this nifty volume isn't as hefty as some? We avoid the unnecessary prattle and give you what you need to know. This way, you can spend more time doing important things like saving the world or catching up on the latest between Brad Pitt and Angelina Jolie. You'll also notice that there are eighteen chapters in this book, just like the eighteen years of your life when you graduate high . . . okay, forget it.

2) **We say what we mean and we mean what we say.** Though we don't claim to have *the magic key* to getting into a certain college (nobody should claim such a thing), we do offer a practical, no-nonsense guide to navigating the mayhem—and with what we'd like to think is a touch of humor. Basically, we intend for this guide to be a sane look at a process that's gone a little haywire. In addition, to make our suggestions more meaningful, we share a number of "real world" examples from both sides of the process—the "before" and "after" of applying—along with a few awkward dating stories. The names of the victims—er, students— will, however, be changed.

3) **Dating and the college admission process really do share some common traits.** As you've already noticed from the cover, we're making an analogy between the wonderful worlds of college admission and, as the Beatles sang, "love . . . love . . . love." Why? So the authors can tap into the lust element of romance and the fear connected with college admission, sell the movie rights, and make a bazillion dollars. Actually, a whole slew of connections exist between the two, seemingly disparate, realities: the wooing, the desperation, the rejection, the hurt ego, the waiting, the sour grapes, the elation . . . you get the idea.

Even the language that students use when looking at colleges sounds familiar. They want to "get noticed" by the "perfect one" while also finding the "right match." After a college visit, they'll say they liked the place on paper, but that it just didn't "feel" right. They long for a school that lines up with their own world view but which will also push them to explore new perspectives. They want a college they'll carry with pride through the rest of their lives. And, most important of all, they want a really good kisser. (Okay, so much for the analogy on that one.)

***Unfortunately, as in the dating world, there's a great deal of un-happiness out there.*** Divorce rates are as ridiculous as ever and many students are stressed and unhappy about the college where they end up. Of course, as in marriage, much of the responsibility for happiness or not lies with the individuals themselves, which is where we step in. We want to arm you with knowledge so you know what you're getting into while we allow you to see that in some instances, loving the one you're with isn't such a bad idea. In short, with a practical approach, ***we hope to demystify some of this process and allow for more fairy tale-endings.*** As with romance, if you go in with open eyes, a good sense of yourself (and humor), and a strong idea about not only what you want but what you need—along with a few do's and don'ts for the journey—you'll be much better off. And maybe, just maybe, when all's said and done, you'll have picked up a thing or two about dating as well. (But don't count it.)

Now, since you probably haven't made your decision about this book yet, flip through the pages, check out the table of contents, and decide for yourself. It'll be a fun ride . . . even if that well-intentioned aunt really is the only reason you're holding it.

## Chapter 1

# The Glamour
# of Falling in Love

### A few thoughts about the hype

> *"The most useful piece of learning for the uses of life is to
> unlearn what is untrue."*
> —ANTISTHENES

We've all seen it in the movies: the passionate embrace, the steamy kiss on the beach, the slow-mo dating montage set to romantic music. And, as we all know, these movie depictions are exactly how relationships play out in reality—just as we know that once we get into the one and only college for us, our lives will be filled with happiness forever and all time.

Okay, you might note the sarcastic tone, but there's a reason for it. We've seen even the most jaded students get caught up in the whole, "If I only make it into Hubba Bubba University, then my life really will be complete. I just know it." *This attitude about college is an attitude that says something about the very essence of human nature itself: we want the things that are just out of reach.* We imagine that once we attain the car/stereo/school/job, *then* we'll be happy, and everything will fall into place.

Some big-name researchers in the fields of psychology, sociology, and economics are now quantifying and confirming this very notion—that people *want* to want. Most people seem eternally stuck in "unsatisfied" mode; indeed, dissatisfaction seems part of our very essence.

Which gets us back to the divorce thing. Along with the high rate of college transfers. And the scary number of middle-aged guys buying red Porsches.

Don't worry, though; this opening salvo isn't intended as any sort of treatise on spirituality in the modern world. It's only meant, rather, to force us all to examine ourselves and our motivations a little more closely. What is it we want, and why do we want it—in the romantic world, in a college, or in anything, for that matter?

At this very moment, you need to throw out any glamorous visions you have about college. Think it's easy? Think you have a realistic view of colleges and the whole admission process already? *Ask yourself this: Have you ever used the word "prestige" when talking about schools? If you have, then you've already bought into the hype.* If you look up the word in the *Oxford English Dictionary*, you'll discover that the definition we typically use today ("blinding or dazzling influence; magic; glamour; influence or reputation derived from previous character, achievements or success") is merely a secondary meaning. The word actually comes from the Latin "praestigium," meaning, quite simply, "illusion," with its full definition being "illusion, conjuring trick; a deception, an imposture." And the adjective "prestigious" doesn't fare any better if examined a little more closely: "practicing juggling or legerdemain; cheating; deceptive, illusory." So the next time someone tells you he's only looking at "prestigious" colleges, you can just smile to yourself because you know better.

But hey, you're thinking, who cares about a little-known piece of etymological history?

The hype, however, goes much deeper. The oft-quoted *U.S. News & World Report* college rankings seem scientifically sound. After all, just look at the impressive rows of statistics lined up neatly, one after another. Such graphics and numbers certainly wouldn't lie, right? Right?? But if you study those same numbers carefully, they'll shift before your very eyes.

Parents regularly come to our offices demanding to know which college is "the best," and they expect an easy, objective answer. "The best for what?" we always ask. But it's often clear they have already fallen under *U.S. News & World Report's* spell. So here's the reality: in the *U.S. News & World Report's* rankings, a large percentage of a school's status is based on "perceived prestige" as voted by other college presidents (there's that "prestige" thing again). So first of all, we're talking about an illusion; second of all, it's a "perceived" illusion; and third, it seems to be an illusion based more on who a college president's golf buddies are than what really goes on in the classroom. The rest of the rankings are based on things like endowment, alumni giving, and student attrition rate, but they have little to do with academic atmosphere or campus culture—in short, characteristics that actually might have a connection to the educational experience. ***There's a smaller ranking called the National Survey of Student Engagement that takes these educational questions into account, but, unfortunately, it's not nearly as flashy or fun to talk about.***

For example, Brown University hasn't always enjoyed its current name cachet. Only a few decades ago, it wasn't nearly as selective—until that is, the admission director began rejecting students who were being admitted to Harvard, Yale, and Princeton and accepting kids who seemed just a bit more original and creative. The result? More interesting graduating classes, along with a big boost in the public eye. Today, Tufts University has a new director of admission who is also reframing how Tufts is perceived by the public. Always a good school, Tufts had been in the shadow of several nearby Ivies. Now, Tufts requires even more thoughtful, creative, and inventive responses on its application and essay. It is no longer taking the "perfect" student who almost got into Harvard and now has a chip on his shoulder; now it wants originality. Already, students are talking about Tufts in a different way.

Image certainly can be related to substance, but still, the majority of the hype is based on empty fluff.

One of the illusory—and icky—aspects of this whole process is that *most colleges* desperately want you to apply to them, even if they know you won't get in. We've had advisees sitting in our offices, shaking their heads, wondering about a rejection notice after the college representative had sent a letter (one of the famous "search" letters) that seemed to encourage their application. "How can this be?" they always ask. "What happened?" But what happened is simple: **The more ap-**

plicants a school receives, the more it can reject, and the more it rejects, the higher it goes in the selectivity rankings. And there's the sleight of hand we mentioned before. (Make sense now?)

Oddly enough, the same students who make gagging noises while watching a romantic scene in a movie, claiming it's too "cheesy" and "unrealistic," can't see that there's a similarly unrealistic cheesiness going on in the process of college admission. *The same students who think they're edgy and on top of things approach the "prestige" schools with a deference approaching awe, but they can't see that they're a pawn in an elaborately-wrought marketing campaign.*

The hype and fear, sadly, permeate virtually every stage of the process. Jumping on the college spring marketing bandwagon are all the "honorary" societies out there. One of Eric's students came to him with a letter that began: "Congratulations. Based on your outstanding academic achievement at your high school, you have been nominated for membership in . . ." Not until four paragraphs later, of course, did the letter mention the $45 "membership fee." The student, who didn't have either great scores or a particularly strong GPA, would have been one more victim to the hype. She thought that filling out the form and sending in the money would have given her that magic edge, but it only would have left her with a little less cash for going out to dinner with friends.

---

### Don't Think There's a Lot of Hype Out There? Consider:

1) The "Ivy League" is simply a reference originally created to describe a sports conference.

2) If you ever get around to reading the article entitled "College Quality and Future Earnings: Where You Should Send Your Child to College," published in *The American Economic Review* (volume 79, #2 May 1989, pp. 247-252), you'll see that where you go to school isn't nearly as important as what you do once you're there. In the long-term study, researchers tracked students who attended the Ivies versus those who were accepted but opted to go somewhere else—maybe a local state school. And how different were these two groups? You wouldn't be able to tell.

3) As Bill Mayher reports in *The College Admission Mystique*, in a number of the "big name" universities, the undergraduates are essentially subsidizing the graduate education—which, in many cases, is where the schools' reputations come from.

4) Ronald Reagan attended Eureka College. (Where? Our point exactly. Whether you admire the Ol' Gipper or not, you probably assumed his alma mater had a more familiar ring to it.) And he's just one of many mucky-mucks who attended a school you probably haven't heard of. James Buchanan attended Dickenson; Jimmy Carter studied at the Georgia Institute of Technology and Georgia Southwestern College (along with Union and the Naval Academy); William Henry Harrison attended Hampden Sydney—right before he dropped out, that is; Benjamin Harrison went to Miami University of Ohio; and Warren Harding attended Ohio Central.

5) There are many excellent lesser-known colleges out there—both public and private—offering fine educations that can boast of high percentages of alums going on to graduate, medical, or law school. Why isn't the whole world talking about these unsung stars? They don't have big sports teams; they have small or nonexistent graduate programs; or maybe their location simply isn't as glitzy. Because they aren't as "selective" as some schools, their "clubs" simply don't seem all that "prestigious," when you come right down to it. See through the hype, and flip to the back of this book for a look at our list of personal favorites.

---

All this, of course, doesn't mean that you should avoid reading *U.S. News & World Report*; read it, but do so along with every other ranking you can get your hands on. Read about the best outdoorsy schools and the happiest schools and the schools where people are most likely to play the ukulele, if that's what floats your boat. Read them all, and see each as having something to offer, for the truth is that they all do.

Of course, this advice is not to discourage your application to some of those brand-name schools. If they're a good match for you (which we'll be talking more about later), then go for it. Just think about why you're really interested and what your goals are.

Also, don't forget that hype and social pressure influence even the likes of you. One theory about why the divorce rate in our country is so high is that many couples come into the relationship with expectations of lovey-dovey schmoopiness forever and all time. While the thought of that is a little disgusting anyway, it's also unrealistic. Practical matters need to be dealt with: personalities, finances, values, and, of course, hair in the sink. The same goes for college, as well (even the hair in the sink part—you might be surprised).

Without even consciously realizing it, you have an image of what a good school is, but you need to ask yourself what that image is based on, exactly. Would it be Reese Witherspoon's attending Harvard in

*Legally Blonde*? Or Tom Cruise sweating it out in Princeton's admission office in *Risky Business*? Or maybe you're more into Will Ferrell in *Old School*? Though no one would say these movies are faithful depictions of reality, the images they create stay with us nonetheless: what college students should look like, how red the bricks in the buildings should be, and how professors should profess. These images, along with what our neighbor's brother-in-law's second cousin said about where he went, form our opinions.

So it all comes down to this: if you understand that the slow-mo dating montage isn't all that relationships are cracked up to be, then you're already on the right track.

> ## How to Tell When You're Falling in Love (Or Maybe When You're Just Coming Down with the Flu):
>
> 1) You can't eat or sleep.
>
> 2) Your stomach is doing backwards somersaults.
>
> 3) Your palms turn sweaty.
>
> 4) You suddenly start liking schmaltzy music.
>
> 5) You can't get any work done.
>
> 6) You find yourself thinking those posters with the kittens on them are cute.

**Chapter 2**

# So . . .
# Who Are You, Anyway?

## The importance of knowing yourself
## with ten questions to help

> *"Philosophy has informed us that the most difficult thing
> in the world is to know ourselves."*
>
> —CICERO

The middle-school dance. Just saying the words conjures up images of awkwardness for most people. Remember trying to act cool while secretly hoping someone would ask you to dance? And the whole time you're standing by the bowl of Cheese Puffs, you're thinking two words: "pick me." You're older now, and the Cheese Puffs have been tossed out, but you're still standing there, still thinking those same two words.

The difference now is that you're not just an amorphous, identity-less, middle-school blob any longer (which we say with only the greatest respect for middle-school students everywhere). You're starting to get a sense of who you are—something that should take an entire lifetime, but you should be really focused on this endeavor right about . . . NOW.

You might know Socrates' dictum about the unexamined life's not being worth living, and, while you don't want to become too self-absorbed, you do need to have a strong sense of who you are.

## THE DREADED ADVICE: "BE YOURSELF."

Maybe you've heard it before heading out on a date you're nervous about. "Just be yourself," some well-intentioned but misguided friend will say. So you smile, nod, and wonder what the heck the phrase really even means.

Though "be yourself" has become a tired cliché, it's still worth considering for its true meaning. As college counselors, we see the "herd" mentality all the time, and colleges fall in and out of favor for no logical reason. So calm down and listen to the real you before rushing into the fray.

Rather than starting with the question, "What do colleges—or, for that matter, future dates—want?" instead, at this stage in the game, you should be asking, "Who am I?" Before you put yourself out there, you've got to have something to talk about.

Filling out bubble sheets on standardized tests or remembering social security numbers, pins, and passwords, it's easy to feel like a number in today's world. During the application process, it's tough not to see ourselves as rosters of activities with names attached. But what beliefs, fears, and yearnings drove those rosters to be created in the first place? If you're only doing the things you do to pad a résumé for college, then you *really* do need to consider yourself in a new light.

Several years ago, a student—let's call her Penelope—animatedly detailed all the writing camps she had attended, describing them as something she was really passionate about, and, like a dope, Eric, her counselor, believed her. Later, when someone asked Penelope if she was going to attend any more camps the summer after senior year, he overheard her respond with a cool, "Why? I'll already be in college by then." Now, perhaps dear, sweet Penelope was merely downplaying her enthusiasm with a peer, but the attitude she expressed was nevertheless lame. If she really had attended the camps only to "look good," she'd find herself struggling even more later on because this is how her life's scenario would play out: in college, she would do what she needed to make it to the next level (job, grad school, whatever), and then she'd find herself scratching her head and wondering, what next? Why? Because she never bothered to stop and wonder who she was.

Similarly, we've all known people who change their behavior dramatically on dates to impress the other person. We're not talking about putting on a clean pair of jeans for a change; that should happen anyway. We're talking about people who act like someone they're not—more sophisticated, less sophisticated, taller, shorter, whatever. "Don't tell her I collect *Star Wars* action figures," he'll say. But why not? This fact of the dating world and college admission is the same: the truth will come out sooner or later.

We've known students who start volunteer projects, and the second they're in college, they abandon them. The students worthy of respect, however, are the ones who do something they really love and stick with it. It's such a part of their life, such a joy, that they don't think of it as something for a résumé.

Though it might seem like other high school students are all winning Nobel Prizes, opening homeless shelters, and finding cures for cancer—and maybe some are—if these things aren't you, then don't feel pressure to do them. Instead, find the thing that really speaks to who you are. If after much thinking, all you can come up with is sprawling on the couch, then you might want to redirect your life just a little.

Some students believe that "being yourself" means contriving a persona that'll be just quirky and odd enough to stand out. If quirky and odd aren't what you're comfortable with, don't do that, either. *The second you start to talk in a completely honest way—the way you do with your closest friends—you'll stop being a cliché and become an individual.* That'll stand out.

## THE SECOND BIT OF DREADED ADVICE: "BE PASSIONATE."

Along with "be yourself," another mantra students frequently hear from colleges is, "Show us you're passionate." Again, this is sounding more and more like dating, but passion is key in both worlds. Who wants to be with a boring dud? What college wants someone whose only function is that of a seat warmer—however good-looking?

A while back, another student—let's call her Isolde—looked glum as she described how the college interview had gone. "They asked some really tough questions," Isolde said, looking down. "Like what?" Eric asked, wondering if she had gotten some of the "Who would you invite to dinner?" sorts of questions. "Lots of things . . ." Isolde mumbled,

"They even wanted to know what *books* I liked." "Oh," Eric said, seriously contemplating lighting his hair on fire.

Obviously, you want to have a few basics covered—with books being at the top of that list; don't, however, feel like you have to prepare a speech on the wonders of *To Kill a Mockingbird*. Chances are, the admission guy found the book as dull as you did. If skateboarding is your thing, maybe you just finished an interesting history about the Dog Boys of Z-town. If you're a foodie, maybe you just read *Kitchen Confidential*. Maybe you disliked the book, but at least you have an opinion about it. Having an opinion means you're thinking.

## HOW TO HANDLE TALKING ABOUT "YOURSELF" AND YOUR "PASSIONS"

So, you want to be yourself and be passionate, but you also need to be able to speak articulately about who you are and what you're passionate about. Some of our favorite students over the years (Wait . . . did we just say that? We love all our students equally!) have confessed how uncomfortable they feel when talking about themselves. "It sounds like bragging," they often tell us. Though you'll certainly need to ixnay any tone of arrogance, the college admission process is one of the few times in your life you can talk about yourself and not worry about the fact that you're . . . well, talking about yourself.

*If you're stressed about coming across as arrogant, that's a good sign because arrogant people typically don't worry about how they come off.* College admission reps can see through people who are full of themselves just as you can often tell within the first few minutes of a date. One friend confided to Eric that she learned a lot about a guy by how he treated the wait staff in a restaurant; and while tipping your admission rep would not be a good idea, being polite without seeming too eager is the right tone to strike.

Another woman—Dulcinea, say—described how a date sat down across from her at the table and began to unload his whole life story, mother issues and all. Thirty minutes later, when she realized she hadn't even gotten a word in edgewise, she politely excused herself to go to the powder room and left the restaurant.

While your admission rep will likely not leave mid-interview, make it easier on him or her by talking about yourself with clear enunciation, answering questions with more than a "yes" or "no," and—get ready—even smiling. Just as Dulcinea's date should have known, you mustn't attack the admission rep with a list of your heroic exploits or tragic failures, but rather assume a conversational tone that you'd use with a teacher. And one more thing: don't forget to *listen*.

Though we'll be talking about essay-writing and interview tips later, this is a general heads up: during the college admission process, as on a first date, show your excitement about what really gets you going, but do so in a way that allows the person listening to breathe.

By the way: almost anything that excites you is fair game. Even if your passion is video games, the fact that they're a multi-million dollar industry means that if you can speak intelligently about them, you'll not be brushed aside. If a school sees that you have drive related to whatever it is you like to do, this speaks volumes.

After all, without drive and passion, Walt Disney would have been just another kid who liked to doodle!

---

### The "Who Are You?" Quiz: Ten Questions to Help You Learn a Little More About Yourself

So, it's all fine and good to talk about "being yourself" and "finding your passion," but how does this translate from the abstract into reality? To start, there are a few specific "to do" queries that'll help you focus. The following are the questions to start asking. (Roll your eyes all you want; answer these questions, and then read the pages that come after to see our enlightening comments. You really and truly might just figure some things out about yourself . . .)

**The Quiz**

1) How do you spend your free time?

2) Where do you see yourself ten years from now?

3) What are you doing now that actually connects to your future goals?

4) What are your plans for this summer?

5) List ten adults you respect, and find out where each went to college.

**Ten Respect-worthy Grownups**

| | |
|---|---|
| 1) | 6) |
| 2) | 7) |
| 3) | 8) |
| 4) | 9) |
| 5) | 10) |

6) How smart are you? (What are your academic strengths and weaknesses?)

7) How organized are you? (Rank yourself on a scale of 1-10, with 10 being the best; then have your parents rank you, too.)

8) How much of a stress case are you? What stresses you out? What do you do to avoid stress?

9) What scares you about the college admission process?

10) What really and truly motivates you? (What's making you want to go to college in the first place?)

Okay, how bad was that? Of course, now that you've mulled over some of these questions, answered some, and ignored others, take a few minutes to read over the commentary related to each question. There's a method to our madness, and we hope to explain it here . . .

### 1) How do you spend your time?

Ask yourself what you do with the majority of your free time, and count how many hours you actually engage in each activity per week. Think back over yesterday, for instance, from the moment you woke up. You might say you're an avid reader, but if the only thing you read was the credits to *General Hospital*, this might not be an accurate statement. While you wouldn't want to admit that Instant Messaging is a passion, if you spent three hours doing it, it sort of is. Those same three hours represent time you could have spent dabbling in interests that make you more . . . well, interesting.

*Write down some of the things in life that bring you happiness—however superficial they might seem.* Yes, this might sound corny, but hear us out. Give yourself ten minutes, and brainstorm a list. Maybe you'll write that you like to drive country roads at night or that you get really stoked about Thanksgiving dinner. Whatever the activity, each says something about who you are. After writing the list, look back over it, thinking about common themes. *Are most of your pastimes solitary, or do they involve other people? Are they passive or active? Do they involve the arts? Nature? Technology?*

Such considerations will direct you in beginning to think not only about college but also about life beyond.

## 2) Where do you see yourself ten years from now?

Maybe you have a very specific goal in mind. We've had students who've rattled off their entire career trajectory as if it were already written in stone. If you're one of these people, you should keep pursuing your goal but also maintain an open mind. These are the years for exploration, and you never know what might turn up between now and college graduation. One student was certain she was going to major in psychology until she suddenly realized that rocks interested her way more than people. Today, fortunately for her would-have-been patients, she's a geologist.

On the other hand, if you're a student who has no clue what sort of job you see for yourself, give up now because all is lost. Okay, not really. Actually, you're in the majority, and the system in the United States is perfect for you. ***Unlike in some countries where students must know their field of study early on, in the U.S., you have the freedom to shop around for majors first.***

To provide you with some career inspiration, maybe glance back at that list of "happy things." You probably already have a sense of whether you'd be good in an office setting or if you'd like working with your hands. As common-sense as some of this might seem, often, in the whirlwind of expectations, it's easy to forget what inspired us in the first place.

## 3) What are you doing now that connects to your future goals?

We love hearing students talk about their dreams of becoming a journalist, working in international relations, or even directing movies. It's always exciting to hear about such dreams . . . until, that is, the same students make it known they're not doing anything related to them in high school. Out of our many students who say they want to go into journalism, only a few actually have worked on the high school newspaper. Of all those with visions of international relations, just a small handful have participated in Model UN. Somehow, these students are under the impression that once they get to college, their career paths will unfold gloriously before them. But as routine as working for the high school newspaper might seem, that's where it all starts; dreams are fine, but doing something about them is what matters. Also, if the activity seems a little mundane now, here's a newsflash: it'll probably seem mundane later, too.

Those students who think they want to be lawyers until they sign up for Mock Trial and realize it's no fun have already saved themselves time and frustration down the road. ***Trial and error, exploration and detours are all part of the process.*** In sum, don't be afraid of false starts, 180 degree turns, and bumps in the road to bliss—the kind of happiness associated with a college major or the kind we all hope to find in love.

### 4) What are your plans for this summer?

Summer plans are related both to your passions and to how you actually spend your time, so it's good to focus on next summer now. If you plan on playing *Halo* until your brains ooze out of your ears, that's probably not the best strategy—no matter how articulate you might be about the experience.

*If you don't already have a few ideas for the summer, now is a good time to think about what you might do.* Service work, sports camps, or even writing a Hollywood screenplay all are great ideas, but, just as importantly, don't feel that you have to fill up every minute with a specific, organized activity. Taking walks, drawing, playing Scrabble, petting your cat, and just plain daydreaming are all very important. As long as you're keeping the mentally passive activities like chilling in front of the tube to a minimum, you're moving in the right direction.

### 5) Who are a few adults you respect?

List the adults you admire, for whatever reason. Maybe you define success through service, achievement in the business world, creativity, or simply just being interesting to talk to. However you define it, though, think of ten adults who match your model. Once you've finished your list, see if you can find out where each went to college. You'll likely be surprised by some of the answers.

While you certainly can include a president or some other famous person if you must, don't forget people close to you: parents, rabbi, teachers, or just friends of the family. This list should be the one that'll help you start laying the groundwork for the rest of the process.

### 6) How smart are you?

Okay, if you saw that question and panicked, you first need to RELAX because it means you're already looking at this whole college admission process as too much of a validation of who you are. We wrote the question because it ties into question #8 related to how stressed-out you are. If, on the other hand, your first thought was, "*very smart*," you might be a little too cocky.

A better question would be: what sort of intelligence do you have? Any teacher with a few years' experience knows there are many types of intelligences in the world, and while some might play better for colleges, each is equally valid in the larger scheme of things.

Maybe you're great at remembering names but terrible at math. Or perhaps music comes easily to you, but reading a history book drives you out of your mind.

To get a sense of how your brain works, look at the subjects in which you do best, and then think about how you study. Do you need to see things in writing? Do you have to hear them? What sorts of tests do you tend to do well on? Knowing these characteristics about yourself will help you start thinking about which college might make a good match.

Considering a school's intellectual climate is crucial. Some colleges are known for kids who love late-night discussions about the meaning of life. One such college, Swarthmore, was visited by a journalist from *Sports Illustrated* who ended up in the football players' locker room after a game. Not only were the players not discussing their loss on the field, he discovered, but they were actually debating Aristotelian philosophy—which, come to think of it, likely explained their loss on the field.

When Lynda toured The University of Chicago, she was struck by the way the students integrate the city's culture into their academic experience. University buses regularly run back and forth to downtown so that it's actually convenient to, say, read a physics assignment at the Art Institute. This may not seem like a big deal, but something as simple as a campus's bus service can parallel that school's larger philosophy.

On a visit to Reed College, Eric noticed in a public restroom, stenciled onto the grout of the tiled wall, the word "groutness"—a play on Platonic thought. Maybe this sort of atmosphere appeals to you, or maybe you find it immensely irritating. Knowing what drives your intellectual curiosity is a big deal because it relates to the school culture you choose. A business major and a philosophy major might both be "smart" dudes, but their curiosities are likely quite different.

Lancelot, a former student and graduate of MIT, recently returned for a visit. "I sort of wish I'd listened to your advice," he said. Eric, you see, had told Lancelot that MIT, wonderful school that it is, might not be the best match for him. "I just miss having people around who like to talk about things other than numbers," Lancelot murmured. Of course, there are many types at MIT (so all you alums, relax!), but Lancelot's desire to go to a school with the status of MIT overshadowed his vision of what a good match for him might be.

Related to all this talk of smarts, of course, is the much-dreaded SAT—the test many see as the final word on how good a brain they have. *If you remember nothing else from this section, remember this: even if your SAT or ACT score isn't where you want it to be, not only are standardized tests NOT an indicator of future life success, but they only speak to a few types of intelligences, anyway.* Speaking of intellectual ability, Eric has a high school friend who bombed every standardized test he touched, but he was also a phenomenal student. He now has two M.A.'s and a Ph.D. from major universities along with a tenured professorship; his SAT score is, of course, only a distant memory. And if you're thinking about success in the business world, you might consider the experience of one of Lynda's friends (yes, we college counselors do have friends!). This gal worried herself sick in high school because her standardized test scores never measured up to those of her older sister. Big sis might have been pretty clever about choosing among multiple-choice responses, but when it came to status, power, and, yes, money, the thoughtful younger sister grabbed the brass ring; she was the very first woman to become a senior vice president in the Fortune 500 company where she ended up working!

One more example of how the multiple-choice test isn't the end-all measure of intelligence occurred in one of Eric's classes several years ago. He'd put up on an overhead projector a cartoon of a boy in a square world with square furniture, square trees, and square-headed parents. The boy had drawn a simple spiral, and his parents were scolding him. The student with a 4.4 average and an almost perfect SAT studied the picture for a moment and made a face. "What is *that* supposed to mean?" she asked. After a moment's pause, another girl, the one happy with a B- and who had barely broken 1000, patiently explained: "It's about conformity . . . can't you see that?" "Are we going to have to know this for the test?" Ms. Perfect Student asked.

The point of all this is to relax and accept how your brain works. One of Lynda's students earned an 800 on the math section, but he wanted to take the test again because he had actually missed two problems—with the moral being, these tests make everyone a little nutty. If you know you're a terrible test-taker, focus on schools that don't emphasize them as much; some don't require them at all, while others offer choices among tests or excuse them for students with a certain GPA. On the other hand, if you shine while blackening ovals with your No. 2 pencil, go ahead and enjoy the advantages high scores can give you, but realize that these numbers are just one aspect of the college application.

---

### Here are a few of the many four-year schools that don't require any standardized testing:

| | |
|---|---|
| Bates College | Bowdoin College |
| College of the Holy Cross | Denison University |
| Dickinson College | Drew University |
| Franklin and Marshall College | Gettysburg College |
| Goucher College | Guilford College |
| Gustavus Adolphus | Hobart and William Smith Colleges |
| Knox College | Lake Forest College |
| Lawrence University | Lewis and Clark College |
| Mount Holyoke College | Muhlenberg College |
| Pitzer College | Rollins College |
| Saint John's College | Saint Lawrence University |
| Union College | Worcester Polytechnic Institute |
| Providence College | |

For a more complete list of SAT/ACT optional four-year universities and more information, visit the FairTest website at www.fairtest.org/optinit.htm. While you're there, be sure to scroll to the bottom of the page for the explanation of what the numbers after the names of some of the colleges mean. For example, some colleges use the SAT or ACT only for placement and/or academic advising while others use it only when the minimum GPA and/or class rank are not met.

---

*Keep in mind that admission offices tend to avoid students who do well on tests but who don't have strong GPA's. Such a disparity suggests only one thing: the dreaded underachiever.* Remember those rankings we've talked about? Well, one basis for establishing them is the percentage of students who graduate from the college in four or five years. Most colleges aren't eager to take risks on candidates who've already proven that they don't do well in their classes.

So do your best on the tests. Take a prep course if you really want to, or if you're disciplined, save a lot of money by buying one of the prep books and practicing on your own at the kitchen table. But remember: it IS just a test, and it's only one piece of the puzzle. One of Lynda's advisees, a strong and thoughtful student, who was also in both her English class and her AP Spanish Language class, suffered a significant drop in her previously top grades during the fourth quarter of her junior year. About mid-May, she finally came to Lynda's office to talk. Turns out, she was taking several hours of test-prep classes every week while trying to keep up with a heavy course load, play on the golf team, and remain involved with a couple of clubs. She confessed that she knew she'd made a bad decision and took steps to turn the situation around—just in time to study hard for final exams, fortunately!

### 7) How organized are you?

As teachers, we frequently hear students who say, "I'm smart; I just don't do the work." "Well," we think, "if you were that smart, you'd know that work is sort of important." A psychologist colleague once told a student that his friends who did best in medical school weren't necessarily the quickest learners, but they were the ones who were the most methodical. *Fulfilling your responsibilities in school, staying organized, and managing a series of tasks are all indicators of how you'll do later on.*

Organization, of course, is vital to success in college. Many students don't do well because suddenly, for the first time in their lives, no one's watching over their shoulder. On the first day of class, while handing out the course syllabus, a professor might mention the big paper due at the end of the semester and not say much about it until the class is almost over. The organized student writes the paper into her or his schedule and begins work on it as soon as possible so that there's plenty of time for all the necessary research, a thoughtful first draft, and careful revisions. The slacker, however, forgets about it until the night before; after an all-nighter, this person produces something that would most appropriately go straight to the recycling barrel.

If you know you need a little pushing, a smaller college with a strong support system would be a good idea. If you're very self-motivated, a bigger state school where contact with your professors is more limited will likely be fine. *Since having a realistic sense of how "on top of things" you are is so important, rank yourself on a scale of 1-10 for organization; then, ask your parents to rank you as well.* Because students tend to rank themselves on the higher end, and parents tend to be a little less generous, your true "rank" probably lies somewhere in between.

Warning: Students who tell people that they could do better in high school but are just not "challenged" need to change their story. People with real intellectual chutzpah will find the means to challenge themselves in any setting, and they won't blame others for their own shortcomings.

Organization is, as you might imagine, a key component to keeping your head on throughout the application process. During the height of application season, one buttoned-up student asked us, "What's everyone freaking out about? Applying to college isn't that big a deal." We had to agree; if you're organized every step of the way, it really *isn't* that big a deal. Be sure to study the next chapter closely; it's all about timing!

## 8) How much of a stress case are you?

*Making an honest assessment of how prone you are to stress is necessary before going too far along on this journey.* Understanding your stress level should play a part in choosing a college because, quite honestly, some schools are known for their cultures of stress. If you're the sort of student who secretly loves that edge, who exults in talking about how many hours you stayed up studying the night before (and some people really do), then you'll feel more comfortable at some colleges than at others. However, if high stress causes you to shut down, realize this and find a place that matches your personality.

From her own college days at Stanford, Lynda remembers asking a young woman who had recently transferred there from Mount Holyoke why she had changed schools. The reply came as something of a surprise to Lynda, who believed she was working awfully hard in her classes. The recent transfer, an excellent student, said she had come to sunny California from the east coast because she wanted a less intense academic atmosphere. She explained that she wasn't looking for a place to goof off (Stanford would not have filled that bill), but she did want to be able to see the occasional movie, sleep in on Sundays, and have a date now and then.

### 9) What are you scared of?

Okay, this question might be a little tougher to answer. It's personal, and, although we're not asking you to turn into your own psychotherapist all of a sudden, it will require you to look a little deeper inside yourself.

During the application process, many students end up uncovering insecurities, worries, and fears about either themselves or their future. Choosing a college, after all, very likely involves making one of your first big life decisions, and it signifies a breaking away from most of what you know.

Initially, most students say they can't wait to get away from home and high school. Once the process actually begins, different attitudes often emerge. One of Eric's students, Cleopatra, kept delaying doing anything about her application; finally, Eric asked her what was going on. After a few moments of "I don't know's," he noticed a tear running down her cheek; then, with head down, she said, "I'm scared." As they talked, Cleopatra confessed that she really was frightened about leaving home and her friends—everything with which she was familiar— and she felt like she was the only one in her class experiencing these feelings. After a long talk, during which Eric assured her that she most definitely was not alone, she left. A week later, Cleopatra had finished all of her applications; the only thing she had needed to get started was to let someone know how she was feeling.

Similarly, another student—let's call him Antony—was also delaying doing anything about college, despite regular reminders about starting his apps. As a tough wrestler-dude, though, Antony was shedding no tears; even still, Eric sensed that Antony, deep down inside, also was scared of "taking the next step." He had done nothing on his apps, and, as of October, he hadn't even thought about which schools he liked. It wasn't until Antony's father walked into his son's room one night, and, in a gentle tone, explained that if Antony didn't want to go to college the following year, he wouldn't have to, and that it would be perfectly fine for him to take some time off to work while he figured things out. The very next day, at 7:00 in the morning, Eric found Antony sitting outside his office. He had stayed up almost all night making charts that listed which colleges he'd be applying to with dates, deadlines, and requirements. Within a matter of days, he'd finished those apps. Antony had been having so much fun in high school that college seemed like a reality he could wait to worry about later.

Another late starter was one of Lynda's advisees, Rochester, who was driving his parents crazy because he wouldn't even talk to them about colleges. Tired of the frantic phone calls, Lynda sat Rochester down for a heart-to-heart. She asked him where his long-time girlfriend, Jane Eyre, was applying, knowing that Jane's high GPA put her in a whole different league as far as selectivity went. Trying to sound casual, Rochester said, "Oh, we'll break up when we go to college." "Why?" Lynda asked. After a moment, Rochester asked, "You mean we don't have to?" This conversation opened the door to the most unusual list Lynda ever helped a student create. This was their strategy: Jane, who went to another high school, was applying to some high-ranking colleges. So, Lynda and Rochester looked for less-selective but good-fit institutions near each one. For example, to accompany Jane's bid to Wash U., Rochester applied to the U. of St. Louis; to match Jane's app to Stanford, Rochester chose U. of San Francisco; and finally, for the winner, Jane's enrollment at NYU netted Rochester for Fordham.

Later, we'll talk about more conventional list-making procedures.

Some might call all three of these students procrastinators, but from our experience, kids don't do things for just as many reasons as they do them. Inevitably, there'll be the student who'll tell us she thinks college is stupid and that she doesn't want to go, but then we'll find out she simply thinks she isn't smart enough and that she's really worried about failing. Or there's the student who thinks he won't be able to make friends or join a fraternity or play on a team. And so on.

The point of all this is, if you find that you're unable to get yourself together with this college thing, you don't need a degree in psychology to think about what's holding you back. Sometimes, just talking about these roadblocks with someone is all you need to get going. One thing we can guarantee in all this, whether your fears involve dating or college, is a simple truth: you are not alone.

## 10) What are you REALLY after?

Motivation is related to fears, but it's worth examining as its own category. In the movie *Bowling for Columbine*, Marilyn Manson observes that much of our consumer society is based on fear. If you have bad breath, you won't have friends, so buy this mouthwash. Acne? Run out and purchase that cream.

It's not a far stretch to see that the same holds true for how some people view colleges. One despondent student, Don Juan, had actually gotten into his favorite school, but he was upset because another, equally selective, university had turned him down.

"But you weren't even excited about going there," Eric reminded him. "What's up?"

Don Juan thought a moment and squaring his glasses on his nose, responded by saying, "I see that acceptance as a validation of all the work I've done, of who I am." The second he said those words, he realized how silly they sounded. But still, the feeling was there: he was letting the colleges determine his self-worth. Because of that single rejection, Don Juan felt he wasn't good enough.

He certainly isn't the only applicant who falls into this trap. A Lynda advisee, Ana, applied early to two colleges—one early application was binding, and the other, to a less selective school, was not. Ana and her family were absolutely counting on an acceptance from the second, and when she was deferred by *both* colleges, parents and Ana called Lynda at home on a Saturday evening. While Ana sobbed into the phone, Lynda could almost hear the parents wringing their hands with worry. Despite Lynda's explanation that a deferral is not a rejection—often a college simply wants to wait to see first-semester senior-year grades before making a decision—and gentle reminders that Ana had other excellent alternatives on her list, Ana wailed that she was a failure. She concluded that she'd worked all through middle and high school for nothing! (By the way, Ana was later accepted by both colleges.)

Then there are the "scalp hunters"—high-achievers who want to be able to brag about the many colleges to which they've been accepted, even though they may never have had any genuine interest in attending most of them. They, too, are allowing an admission committee to rate them in terms of what they're worth. Besides that, they may actually harm their classmates because some colleges will only admit a limited number from any given high school. One kid's extra acceptance may mean that someone else, for whom that college was actually the top choice, loses out.

The kids aren't the only ones who fall into this trap. We've had parents, who feel their social standing depends on where their children attend college, ask us which preschool their child should go to because they think that will have repercussions related to the elementary school, high school, and, you guessed it, college. Not long ago, a high-powered Wall Streeter was nabbed for sharing insider information, and why? So he could be assured his two girls would be admitted into an elite New York preschool. The only result was that he was admitted to a not-so-elite jail.

You could say that one of the primary motivations in all this is fear, but this particular fear comes from a need for status, which in turn is based on one simple desire: to be noticed and admired by other people.

When students say they're applying to both Princeton and Brown, it might seem as if they're more focused on the school names than anything else because those two schools are quite different from one another. *Likewise, when students say they're applying to any big-name university, but the only reasons they can come up with are that "it's a good school and everyone's heard of it," we can only suppose they're trophy-hunting, too.* If, however, a student speaking about the same school can say that she likes the astrophysics department there or that she knows the study abroad program to Chile offers terrific options, she gains a lot of credibility; we know these kids are applying for the right kinds of reasons!

In the same way that some guys hit a mid-life crisis and marry a trophy wife half their age, some students fall into the trophy-hunt for bumper stickers with the right college names. One of Eric's students refused even to look at a particular college because she couldn't imagine its name on her sweatshirt.

*Related to status, some people choose their college because they see it as a logical move—as if they were playing chess.* By going to Dipsydoodle U., they'll be assuring their future lifelong success, even if they don't really like the place all that much. As we mentioned earlier, in that *American Economic Review* study, this does not typically prove to be the case. There are little colleges like St. John's College in Annapolis and Santa Fe that can boast spectacular success rates for their students in grad school because of their rigorous but supportive academic programs. On the flip side, some top-notch grad schools like to see students who've risen in the ranks at big state universities because it means they're self-motivated and responsible.

One of Lynda's former advisees, thoughtful Romeo, attended Yale, the most selective of the six colleges where he'd applied. In his heart, though, he had wanted to attend the much smaller Colorado College because he liked the one-course-at-a-time block plan that would have enabled him to focus his efforts intently. At Yale, he worked so hard that he missed out on some great aspects of college life, and even so, he earned more B's than A's. Spread thin, he just didn't really stand out there; as a result, he was rejected by every medical school to which he applied.

On the other hand, another of Lynda's former advisees, brilliant Juliet, had her pick among a number of "hot-shot" universities, but, after careful deliberation, she chose instead to be a "big fish in a smaller pond" at perfect-fit Brandeis. There, she earned rock-star grades and was taken under the wings of several professors; she reported back that she was doing some terrific independent research as a sophomore. Juliet, as you might guess, got the coveted "thumbs-up" from 13 of the 15 med schools she applied to.

Romeo's story reveals that emotion can end up ruling out over logic. One afternoon, the father of one of Eric's students confessed that he really wanted his son to attend Princeton. Knowing that this father was one of the country's most respected emergency room doctors, Eric asked him why Princeton, specifically. Dad responded with a simple, "It'll help my son get into the medical school he wants."

At this point, knowing this particular father's history, Eric played his hand: "And where did you do *your* undergrad work?" he asked innocently. Knowing where Eric was headed, the father paused, and clearing his throat, said, "Okay, I see your point." He had attended Adelphi College.

Beyond status, mob mentality affects how some students approach their college "research." "What have you read about Ding-Dong University?" we'll ask. The student will begin with, "Uh . . . nothing really, but my mom's friend said her son's girlfriend liked it. *It's fine to listen to what people say, but do your own investigating.* At many high schools, once one college gets "noticed" by a few students, what we call "the lemming effect" takes over, and large numbers of kids start applying there. If you remember that just because a lot of people apply to a place doesn't make it better, you'll be happier.

Don't be afraid to strike out on your own. At one time in the dark past, there was a spot in our upper school hallway called "the senior corner" because, as you probably have guessed, that's where the seniors hung out between classes. It was also where there was a lot of buzz about colleges. One of Lynda's advisees, doing just the kind of investigating that we encourage, went with her mom to visit The University of Puget Sound because she'd read that there were terrific Pacific Rim courses there. After the trip, both the girl and her mother felt that UPS was a very good fit and told Lynda so. A couple of days later, though, the student showed up in Lynda's office with tears streaming down her face. Seems as though nobody in the senior corner had "heard of" UPS (remember, this was a while ago), and of course they thought it couldn't merit an application. Fortunately, the student listened to her own voices, attended UPS, loved it, and spread the word. Guess which college is now super-popular among many of our students?

I THINK YOU'RE A LITTLE YOUNG TO START THINKING ABOUT DATING AND LIPSTICK, SWEETIE...

OK, MOM.

## Chapter 3

# Timing Is Everything

## The calendar

*"He who is not impatient is not in love."*
—PIETRO ARETINO

How a person approaches dating is often similar to how he or she approaches the college admission process. Some see both as a race to be won, with either college acceptance or the perfect mate as the ultimate goal, and a goal one can't start working toward early enough. Later on in life, these same people will lament their lack of time, complaining that their "biological clock" is running out or that everyone else is way ahead of them.

To these people, we say one word: chill. Of course, saying this to such a person never helps: it only feeds the fire. Often our over-stressed students inform us that our telling them to relax only makes them start thinking about all the reasons why they *shouldn't* relax, and then they think perhaps we know some other reason why they shouldn't relax, which is really why we're telling them to do it in the first place. Whew.

Similarly, we've seen friends in the dating world settle for marriage partners because they simply felt they were running out of time. They had to do everything yesterday. For some, dating is a serious endeavor with a clear set of objectives, and quite frankly, it doesn't involve much fun, nor does it have a lot to do with love. Each date can turn into a job interview that forms part of an ongoing candidate search.

We've already talked about some of the students on the other end of the spectrum who, for one reason or another, are paralyzed by fear and can't get started, but then there are students who are so caught up in enjoying their high school years—remember wrestler-dude Antony?—that they figure sometime around graduation they'll get around to filling out an application. The dating equivalent of both these types of procrastinators could be the commitment-phobe who never gets serious with anyone because playing the field is so much fun and not nearly so scary as settling down.

The best place to be, as you might imagine, is somewhere between these two zones, between the non-starters and the racers. The college admission process should be a tool for self-discovery, and it can also be a time in your life that's sort of fun. After all, you're picking the place where you'll be living and studying for the next four (or so) years, along with determining the direction of the first stage of your adult life.

Similarly, dating, too, can also be a tool for self-discovery, and it should also be fun. You're figuring out what sort of person you most like to be with, and that tells you a lot about yourself.

So the advice here is not to start too early, but to begin early enough that you never feel overwhelmed. Parents have walked into our school's college counseling office, wondering why they haven't received any information about applying to college.

"Because your child is still only *eleven*," we'll tell them. All such a parent hears is, "blah blah blah, you're running out of time." Now, if you're the son or daughter of one of these parents, what follows is a timeline for the college admission process that you can use if anyone—including you—starts to panic.

## TIMELINE

**Freshman year in high school:** Do well in classes. Join a club or two. Play a sport you enjoy. Read good books. Get to know your teachers. Have nice friends. Climb a mountain. Play with your cat. Enjoy your summer vacation.

**Sophomore year:** Take the classes that your teachers and counselor recommend. When you have choices, take on some challenges, but don't go for so many honors courses that your workload overwhelms you. Devote yourself passionately to a few activities, choosing only the ones you really care about. Read more good books. Get culture: go to a museum; see a play; attend a concert (not limited to the rock variety). Do something that helps someone else. Don't worry about having lost some of your freshman-year friends: they were knuckleheads anyway. Swim in the ocean. Play with your dog.

If you've been following our advice, by the end of your sophomore year, you've established yourself as a respected member of your class, academically and socially. You may be ready to head a committee, run for an office, or talk about something that really interests you. You've gotten to know some of your teachers because you're a dependable, responsible student. You've chosen a sensible but challenging course load for junior year, and you aren't going to waste your summer sleeping until noon every day. Maybe you've got some great baby-sitting or lawn-mowing jobs; maybe you'll help build a house with Habitat for Humanity; maybe you'll attend a sports camp. Save time to read more of those good books and take long walks, though.

Some of our students feel as if an SAT or ACT prep course needs to be part of that summer after sophomore year. We don't think so—with one exception. If you're that rare person who was born to excel on standardized tests, go ahead and prep for the PSAT. The very top scorers on that test, which is offered in October of the junior year, go on to be recognized by the National Merit Corporation. Being a Merit Scholar doesn't mean that you're set for life, but it can grease the skids a little as you apply to colleges and provide some scholarship funds.

**Junior year:** Fall of the junior year is a good time to push yourself even harder in classes. Colleges will have a long, hard look at junior-year grades, and you'll very likely be asking some of these teachers to write recommendations for you. Take the PSAT in October, whether or not you're a terrific test-taker. The "P" stands for "preliminary," but it also means "practice." You can sign up with your counseling office, and you can also get free sample test materials. Use them to understand the different kinds of questions on the test. When you get the PSAT results, figure out what you're doing right and what sorts of questions cause trouble for you. This will help you decide whether or not you want to do test prep and what kind of prep might make sense for you.

This is also an excellent time to work on that whole business of self-discovery. (Review the questions you just answered in the previous chapter!) Are you a great baseball catcher? Do Amnesty International's causes fire you up? Do you love performing in the school's big musical? Do you like getting together with other French Club members to make éclairs and watch *Amelie*? Does it make you feel good to tutor a younger student who's struggling in math? You won't need a list of ten activities when you apply to college, but you do need to involve yourself with the life of your school's community.

Related to this, have you thought about community service? If you haven't, do, and if you have, make sure you find something and stick with it—and something you actually like, too. Don't be the kid with *The Onion* article headline: "Soup-Kitchen Volunteers Hate College-Application-Padding Brat." Though the story, like the newspaper, is a spoof, the sentiment hits closer to home than you might know. Don't be *that* kid, the one the real volunteers shake their heads and grumble about.

Most students start thinking pretty seriously about the college selection process sometime during the middle of the junior year. Maybe it's seeing all the seniors talking about lists and apps and essays, or maybe it's just part of growing up. It probably makes sense to start looking at some college books (the one you're holding now, for example) and visiting some specific college websites so that you can learn more about the process and the many *types* of schools that are out there. If there's a college or two located near you, then fit a tour and an information session into your schedule. If you're spending a holiday at your grandmother's house in Dallas, visit Southern Methodist University, Austin College, and Texas Christian University while you're in the area. If your family goes to SeaWorld in San Diego, tour the University of San Diego and the University of California, San Diego.

ACT, SAT, SAT Subject Tests, and AP Exams likely belong somewhere in the second half of the junior year, and it's also a good time to sit down with your parents and counselor to start building a preliminary list of schools for investigation. Decide on a couple of teachers you'd like to write college recommendations for you, and ask them nicely if they'll do it. Consider running for an office in your favorite club or your class or even your student body! If you might be eligible to play Division I sports, register with the NCAA Clearinghouse. Sign up for a challenging but sensible senior-year course load, but caution: applying to college takes about as much time as a class during fall semester!

The summer after your junior year is the time to power up on all fronts. Start your own Fortune 500 company, win the US Open, cure AIDS . . . Okay. Just kidding. But do review our advice for the summer after sophomore year, and take it all up a notch. This could also be primo test-prep time—you'll have the opportunity to re-take the SAT, the ACT, and SAT Subject Tests in the fall of your senior year. Visit some of the colleges that interest you. Brainstorm essay ideas for your college apps. Again, though, save some time to have a life and be human.

**Senior year:** It's show time! Most of the following speeds up if you're applying Early Decision or Early Action or even rolling (more about this later), but basically, here's the schedule. Organization (yes, we know we already talked about this subject) is essential to making the process go smoothly:

### September:

- Start your classes on a strong, positive note. Many admission reps say this semester is the best indicator of college success.

- Politely remind the teachers who've agreed to write your recommendations that yes indeed, you're applying to college. Keep these nice people in the loop.

- Sign up for any testing you'll want to do (or re-do) for your apps.

- Get a copy of the Common Application, on-line or from your counseling office.

### October (and into November):

- Go to college fairs, and see the reps from colleges of interest when they come to your high school. Using your best manners, introduce yourself to these visitors. Follow up with thank-you notes.

- Take the tests you signed up for.

- Refine your list of colleges and make decisions about EA, ED, and rolling. Make a clear list of requirements and deadlines for each one.

- If you're thinking ED (binding), be sure to visit that college at a time when you can attend classes and spend the night in a dorm before you make a final decision about applying.

- Do other college visits as time and money permit.

- Work on your apps, whether or not your first deadline is in November.

- Learn about financial aid requirements if you're applying for aid.

- Get recommendation forms to your counselor and to your teachers well in advance of the deadline. (See chapter 9 for how to process the reference-letter paperwork.)

- Request that your school send your transcript and that the testing agencies send your test scores to the schools where you're applying.

- Remember: if you're applying to the U. of California system, you need to do so during the month of November.

**December:**
- Put the finishing touches on all your apps—this will mean doing all supplements for the colleges that accept the Common Application and filling out the apps for the schools that don't accept the Common.

- If you're applying for financial aid, your parents and you should start work on the Free Application for Federal Student Aid (FAFSA).

- Write good thank-you notes to your teachers and counselor, and give each of them a small but thoughtful gift.

- Do a great job on end-of-semester projects and exams.

**January:**
- Request that mid-year reports be sent to your colleges.

- Avoid senioritis.

- Submit the FAFSA if you're applying for aid.

**February and March:**
- Waiting time . . . stay in touch with the colleges and continue to avoid senioritis. Maintain focus on courses and activities.

- Have you thanked your teachers yet?

**April:**
- The good news and maybe some less-than-good news arrive about acceptances.

- An additional visit or two may be in order to help with decision-making.

- Prepare for AP exams in May.

- Notify the lucky school you've decided to attend, and send the deposit by the end of the month. Inform (very politely and in writing) other colleges that accepted you that you're not coming.

**May:**
- Gear up for the big finish, doing your best on all your projects and exams.

- Arrange to have your final transcript sent to the college you'll attend.

**June:**
- Graduation! Congratulations!

## THE NUTS AND BOLTS DOUBLE-CHECK LIST

1) Take the SAT or ACT and Subject Tests any time from junior year on.

2) Get to know your counselor.

3) Research schools.

4) Make your list of colleges.

5) Check to see which schools take the Common App.

6) Fill out the Common App as well as institution-specific applications.

7) Don't forget the supplements.

8) Request that your transcript be sent.

9) Have the College Board and/or ACT send your test scores.

10) Hand teachers addressed, stamped envelopes for each of your schools, along with the reference form for each. Make sure you've waived the right to see the letter.

11) Send app with essay and payment.

12) Do the FAFSA if financial aid will be an issue.

13) Make sure materials arrive at the admission office. (But don't panic if not initially there; the processing takes time.)

**Thought for the day:** Your high school social scene is not a reflection of how your social life will be as an adult; the pendulum of cool will have had its chance to swing back in the opposite direction—trust us (and just look at Bill Gates).

# Checking Out the Field
## Knowing your resources

> *"It would be interesting to know what it is we are most afraid of.*
> *Taking a new step. Uttering a new word."*
> —DOSTOEVSKY

Eric knows a guy—not him, he promises—who, after college, complained about the fact that he only met club-girls who liked to party and drink but didn't have much else to offer a relationship.

"Where are you meeting these girls?" Eric asked.

"Clubs, mostly," the friend said.

Similarly, if you limit your college research to only a few sources—such as what your friends say—you'll be limited in the sorts of schools you find. We often like to show our advisees author Frederick Rugg's list of "favorite" colleges, based on rankings from over 1,000 college counselors. We explain to them the list was compiled by people who know great schools, all hype aside. The students will recognize a number of the names, but the majority, inevitably, will be entirely new.

"*These* are some of the best?" students will ask.

We nod.

The point is, read and research and expose yourself to as much information as possible. Also, remember that while there's more than one soul-mate person out there for you (with all apologies to the hopeless romantics), there's also more than one college.

In the dating world, as you grow older, you'll find your dating resources somewhat limited. You can meet someone at a bar or, on the other end of the spectrum, at church. Of course, there's also the work place, which isn't always a good idea. Since finding the right person can be tough, there exists an entire industry to assist the courtship process, with online dating services, singles luncheons, and even speed-dating being a few. (As a high school student, you're rolling your eyes now, but just wait . . .)

Friends who have met people online often come back from a date, saying the real people were nothing like their description, or even the photo. This can be true with colleges, too, so you'll need to research more than what just the glossy viewbook says. Vary your sources, and read, then read some more. To begin to get an idea of what's out there, here's where you can start looking . . .

## INDEPENDENT COUNSELORS

Just as there are high-priced dating services out there, so, too, are there high-priced counselors for college admission. But please note: precisely as no book, not even this one, has "the secret" to getting into college, no independent counselor does, either. Some will practically promise your admission to an "elite" school, but such promises are meaningless. Not only do these independent counselors not have any special "in" with admission offices, but colleges should never officially know that one is helping you. Your high school counselor is the one who sends your transcript and writes a recommendation letter; the independent counselors can do neither. We're not against all independent counselors, but we're against those who act like mercenaries by tapping into the fear that you can't do this college thing on your own, resulting in their charging way more than anyone reasonably should. There are, of course, a number of good independent counselors on the market, but you should only consider working with one if you attend a high school that leaves you feeling lost in the college selection process. The good independent counselors will not make excessive promises, and they won't act like they have any special information or "in" with schools; they will, rather, act as subtle guides, offering support and making suggestions. If you feel you need an independent counselor because you need someone to hold your hand through every step of the application process and nudge you along, then honestly, you might not be ready for college. Finally, if you're reading these words right now, you have all the independent counseling you need!

Now, we say all this with no disrespect to the reputable and hard-working independent counselors out there, people who legitimately want to guide students through the process and earn a living, too. We only mention this because, with the increasing pressure to "get in," the number of scammers and slackers trying to ride the money wave will only grow, as well.

If you already have a good relationship with your high school counselor, the independent counselor will usually end up muddying the water. First, many of the high-powered independent counselors push kids to create scrubbed, perfect-looking packages that leave the colleges a tad suspicious. After all, having someone else prep your application is almost as creepy as putting a picture of someone better looking than you online in the hopes of getting a date. Second, we have seen firsthand the sort of terrible counseling some of these money-grubbers dish out. One of these nameless individuals was a local, famous among high school counselors in the city for her high-priced bad advice. The situation became worse, however, when she got her hands on our school's mailing list and used it to send out her own promotional material, falsely associating herself with the school.

Just as bad, though, was the nationally-recognized, big-name, big-book author who deigned to write an initial list of schools for one of our students (we found out later). Mr. Big Shot charged the kid the price of a decent used car, and then, in return, gave him a list any schmuck on the street could have come up with. This list, it's important to note, had tons of big name schools, all of which were long shots for this particular student, but they weren't even places that had much in common with him. Of course, Mr. Big Shot didn't care: he had his check (or briefcase of unmarked bills, more like it), and he knew that pumping a student up was the easy part. Of course, he left us holding the "let's be more realistic" bag. Initially, we looked like the bad guys, and how could we not? Here's a big-name dude with nothing to lose, telling you to go to all the big-name schools, so suddenly your high school counselor seems to be underselling you. The kid in this situation caught on and dropped Mr. Big Shot—who is, we'll have you know, still out there, more reputable and "prestigious" than ever.

## YOUR HIGH SCHOOL COUNSELOR

This is the REAL person you want to get to know. Depending on what sort of school you go to, your counselor may or may not be that involved. If you're asking yourself, "*what* counselor?" then you definitely need to read this book closely. If, however, you attend a school which boasts great counselor-student relationships, then this book will simply reinforce and support the two of you as you work together. Eric's own high school guidance counselor wasn't much of a "match-maker." Overwhelmed by too many students, he had a simple response when Eric went to him for advice about college: "If you're staying in-state, we've got some brochures around the corner. If you're going out-of-state, good luck." That was it. On the other hand, Lynda, who also attended a big public high school, got great advice and support from her dedicated, kindly, and overworked counselor. Regardless of the sort of school you attend now, get to know this person. Drop by and say "hi." Even if he or she can't be that hands-on, you'll at least be more than a name and number.

But what, exactly, does this high school counselor do? The image still exists that we counselors have secret "ins" with colleges, and with just a word or a nod, we can get a place to take anyone—even you. This might have been the case a few decades ago, with a certain cadre of high schools and colleges, but the field is much more open now, and counselors are really and truly only guides in this process.

Counselors will often call colleges for status reports about their seniors. They do this so they can, as clandestinely as possible, begin prepping the student if the news is bad. While some colleges don't say anything, others can be very forthcoming. Regardless of what the counselor hears, though, this news is CONFIDENTIAL, so don't even try to pry it out of him or her. Occasionally, conversations will happen, but there is no magic word spoken or arm-twisting. If you're a kid who's below the bar for a certain college, why should a counselor push you? Sure, you're special, but so is everyone else (okay, maybe not that kid who sits behind you in math). And the kid for whom everyone was bending over backwards to get noticed? He's probably not happy at the college anyway, so he transfers. The following year, that same admission officer will be a little less ready to believe that particular college counselor.

No one wins.

If a college will talk to a counselor at all, it's more of a "what else can you tell me about so-and-so?" conversation. Recently, Eric was talking with a college about a student when he realized the admission officer, so overwhelmed by work, might not have given as careful a read to one student as she should have.

"Do you have any questions about Pat?" Eric asked.

"I have his stuff right here. His essay looked fine. He likely won't be an admit, though."

"I understand," Eric said. "However, 'Pat' is actually 'Patricia,' and I just wanted to make sure we're talking about the same student."

"Oh my goodness, I'm SO sorry," the rep blurted out.

Of course, such things happen, but that opening allowed Eric to share a little more about the student.

"I know she might look sort of like this Perfect Stenographer sort of kid, a little tightly wound, but she actually gets that she's like that. She's in on the joke."

Eric shared one short, funny story that had recently involved Pat, and that was it. Eric still figured she wouldn't get in, and that week, he began going over good-bet schools with her, just to be safe.

Amazingly, the student got in. The one, slightly off-putting note to the story is that Patricia wouldn't have, nor could she have, any idea about that phone conversation. She came to Eric, and though not saying so directly, seemed to suggest, "See? You didn't think I could do it, and I did!"

The only reason this "p.s." is worth mentioning is because we've talked to many counselors with similar experiences. They're the ones going to bat for you—again, not bribing or cajoling or anything of the sort, but simply making sure the admission officer knows who you are as a person. Sometimes it helps, sometimes not, but ALWAYS these counselors deserve your appreciation.

A local counselor recently told us how a kid came to her after he'd gotten in to a very choosy school, saying, "I did it, and you low-balled me, not thinking I could. What do you think about *that*?" Of course, what the counselor was thinking about was that the kid was more of a brat than she'd realized, and maybe she shouldn't have gone out of her way as she had to talk about that particular kid's tough family situation and all he'd been through. In the kid's eyes, she had merely been an obstacle.

If you pick up nothing else from this section, remember this: thank your counselor in a genuine and meaningful way—NOW!

## BOOKS

There are tons of college-related books in stores, but you already have one that provides (and we say this in all modesty) excellent general guidance. There are a few others that are great resources for learning about specific colleges. Note: many are filled with fluff or even misguided information, so just because a book has a cute title (and many do), don't assume it's necessarily on the up and up. There are many books that provide a specific focus. The following are simply a few of our personal favorites for general reference:

- *Colleges That Change Lives*, **by Loren Pope**—This book is one we love. Loren Pope, a true guru in the world of college admission, has been providing college guidance for decades now, and his primary theme is simple: find a college that is a genuine match. He wrote *Colleges That Change Lives* because, simply, he saw many students attending colleges where they weren't happy. In the book, he highlights a small cadre of schools that are unique, and unfortunately, often off the typical high school student's radar. While Pope states clearly that these schools are "not for everyone," it is just the uniqueness of their values that makes them worth checking out for some. This book has everything from small, "nurturing" institutions for the student who hasn't quite hit his or her potential in high school yet to places for the people who already know they're intellectual heavy-hitters. You can check out the CTCL website at http://www.ctcl.com for information not only about the book but also the cities the consortium visits when on tour.

- *Rugg's Recommendations on the Colleges,* **by Frederick E. Rugg**—*Rugg's* provides great lists of majors. If you have any inkling as to the sorts of areas of study you might be interested in, this book is a good place to start.

- *The Best 368 Colleges,* **by The Princeton Review**—This is one everyone knows. It provides some good, basic sound-bites in a highly accessible format.

- *The Fiske Guide,* **by Edward Fiske**—This book is similar to *The Princeton Review,* but it provides more of a narrative approach. Just so you know, a number of our students have also found it to be one of the most accurate in its descriptions.

- *The Insider's Guide to the Colleges,* **by Yale Daily News Staff**—This one is a gossipy, fun read, but it's also filled with useful information about the academic and social lives at colleges. Once you're interested in certain schools, look them up here to see what the Yalies have to say about them.

## ONLINE SOURCES

Don't underestimate what you can find on-line; there are websites offering information in scores of categories (Christian colleges, tree-hugging schools, and so on). Of course, if you go to the school's official website, you'll see exactly what the admission office would like you to see: a photo of good-looking, multi-ethnic students sitting under a tree in autumn—with, we can't forget, their bearded professor. Of course, they're all holding philosophy books, and of course, they're all smiling, filled with the joy of learning. From this official website, however, you can also find information that's actually useful. For example, look at the departments for your possible majors. If you like geophysics and you see that there are only two professors in this field—neither of whom focuses on your specific area of interest—that tidbit is sort of important. Also, look at the school's newspaper and connected student sites to get a sense of the cultural climate.

Beyond school-based sites, consider taking a look at The University and College Accountability Network, located at www.ucan-network.org or the College Navigator, www.nces.ed.gov/collegenavigator. Also, don't forget "Nessie," or the National Survey of Student Engagement, which bases its report on what college freshmen and seniors say. Though only around 250 colleges comprise this survey, it still serves as a nice antidote to the *U.S. News & World Report* college rankings.

A few sites for checking out schools:

- www.universities.com

- www.gocollege.com

- www.collegeview.com

- www.petersons.com

- www.campusvisit.com

- www.collegenet.com

- www.blackenterprise.org

- www.hispaniconline.com

- www.catholiccollegesonline.org

- www.hillel.org

- www.christiancollegementor.com

(As you can see, there are websites for college searches related to pretty much whatever you want . . .)

## RANDOM PEOPLE

Once people hear you're a junior or senior in high school, you'll learn—if you haven't already—that everyone has an opinion about college; this is true because everyone, somehow, is also an expert. Most adults who attended college think they have the college thing all figured out, and even if they've just met you, they don't mind telling you so. Of course, just as people you couldn't care less about will give you dating advice in the future, so too, will people you care even less about regale you with college advice. Now, most adults just want you to check out their own alma mater, and if that's the case, listen politely, and if the person is nice, maybe check the school out later. *Just remember one thing regarding advice from all those miscellaneous folks: take EVERYTHING with a grain of salt.* Students have told us how cashiers at supermarkets, uncles, and random dudes at the coffee shop have all tried to impart some sort of wisdom about college. You don't have to blow it all off, but just keep in mind that you don't need to take it all seriously, either. Several years ago, a student, Persephone, just returned from visiting a wonderful all-women's college.

"How'd it go?" Eric asked her.

"Not well," Persephone said glumly.

"Why not?"

"I don't know," she said. "The visit was okay, it was just . . ."

"Just *what*?" Eric probed a little more and discovered that her visit had been ruined before she'd even arrived. A buttoned-up-looking business guy was seated next to her on the flight, and as one might expect, he soon figured out she was a high school student applying to college. "Hmm . . . where are you looking?" he asked innocently enough, but revving himself up to be the wise Purveyor of Knowledge. Persephone mentioned the name of the place. "Oh . . . *there*?" he said with a dour expression. "No offense, but all the girls there are *bitches*. You definitely don't want to go that place." Poor Persephone had to look out the window so Mr. Business-dude wouldn't see her tears, and though she had no problems during her actual visit, she couldn't get his words out of her mind. What sort of experience had her newfound plane friend had with the school? More than likely, a girl who went there had dumped him twenty years earlier, and he was still having a tough time getting over it.

## ALL THOSE PAMPHLETS YOU GET IN THE MAIL

As part of the marketing blitz that colleges begin in the spring, they like to inundate students with brochures, booklets, catalogues, and DVD's. And yes, most look identical, but you might not want to throw them away immediately. If you're organized, you could begin by categorizing the ones that catch your eye—perhaps by region, or even by size. Obviously, you'll eliminate some schools immediately because of class offerings or where they're located; for the others, though, you might just find some hidden gems. Without a doubt, we've had students discover some great colleges they might not otherwise have ever heard of.

### Top Places to Meet Dates

1) In an airport

2) At the supermarket

3) At the laundromat

4) At church

5) In a club

6) In class, the person sitting next to you (but don't look now . . .)

UMMMM...

I MADE A SPREADSHEET WITH THE QUALITIES—HEIGHT, HUMOR, INTELLIGENCE, FAVORITES—OF ALL THE GUYS IN OUR GRADE...

**Chapter 5**

# Setting up
# Your Little Black Book

## Creating a balanced list of good matches

*"To be sure, a love match was the only thing for happiness . . ."*
—MARIA EDGEWORTH

So you've done your research. You've read until you can't read any more, you've checked out school websites online, you've visited and toured, and you've listened to your Uncle Bruce's tales of college merriment from back in the sixties for the zillionth time. Now what?

It's time to make the list. While some people enumerate the "pros" and "cons" of the sort-of-special someone they're currently dating, lists, in general, are best kept out of the realm of romance. For your college search, however, the list is an absolutely vital tool.

The list is designed to help you narrow your odds, but it is not simply a way to apply willy-nilly to tons of schools; rather, a good list involves only colleges you're seriously interested in, and it helps gauge your chances of admission.

Now, this advice of applying only to schools you're "seriously interested in" might seem like common sense. It's not. In today's amped-up feeding frenzy that is the college admission process, many students just apply to entire gaggles of schools, many of which they're only *vaguely* interested in. They do this because they think they're strategizing; they figure that if they throw enough pasta at the wall, some of it's gotta stick (or something like that). Every year, however, we'll find a student in our office looking downcast. "I got into College U," the kid will say. "Why, that's great," we respond. "Let's blow up balloons for the party." But the student will remain somber, and we'll know, but we still need to hear the news directly: "I don't even really want to go there," he or she will inevitably say. Of course, it's at this stage in the college-counseling process when we, as counselors, want to run far, far away and find a new life, maybe as beachcombers on a deserted island. Instead, we smile and respond as we always do: "Well *why* did you apply in the first place?" To this the student will mumble a litany of lame justifications that make no sense.

**Sure, the college admission process is more competitive than ever before, but one of the reasons is that so many students are applying haphazardly to so many schools.** In other words, the stress-cases are creating more stress. If everyone tones things down a notch and applies only to schools they're *seriously interested in* (hear that line again?), the frenzy will die down. If you can, try to think of every college on your list as your "first choice" for one reason or another. For example, maybe one has the nicest dorms, another a beautiful campus near the beach, another a brand new theater, and yet another the best hockey team in its league. We'd hope they all boast some excellent academic offerings, too!

**By the way, before you knock yourself out about the whole competition thing, keep this little nugget in mind: most of the craziness with the college admission process involves the same thirty to forty schools.** Think about the colleges that everyone in your high school talks about. It's a pretty limited group, right? Well, those colleges are the same places everyone else in the country is discussing.

Students will come into our office and tell us that they want a school: "Not too big, but not too small; not too urban, but not too rural; some good school spirit, but also academic. By the way, there should be mountains, the beach, four seasons, and a warm climate." They sound like Goldilocks right before she ticked off the three bears. If you've done your research like we mentioned in the last chapter, you'll have more direction than these more empty characteristics will provide. Heck, saying, "not too big but not too small" is sort of like saying, "I want to go out with someone not too tall but not too short." Vague and bland.

You know, then, to put only SPECIAL colleges on your list. **What's a good number of schools to apply to? We've had students apply to only one or two, and then there are the hyperkinetic stress baskets who mail off twenty apps. If we were to suggest a good number, it'd be between six and nine.** This would allow for two or three applications in each category: "good bets," "targets," and "long-shots." Todd Horn, the headmaster at Kent Denver and terrific teacher of business/econ, advises students to operate as if they were investment bankers needing to diversify their portfolios by creating a diverse list of colleges. Based on your GPA and test scores, you should have a few colleges on the list where you're very likely to get in, or the good bets; a few where you're right in the middle, the targets; and a couple that are super-selective but worth an application because they have something terrific to offer you, the long shots. Lynda likes to think of these classifications in terms of percentages (use your GPA and test scores in comparison with the school's profile as a rough guide here):

- *Good bets*—You have an 80%-90% chance of getting in.

- *Targets*—The odds are 50-50 that you'll be accepted.

- *Long shots*—These schools are so selective and arbitrary that it's virtually impossible to predict who'll be admitted; we can call this a 10% or less chance.

Early in the season, most students come to us with a huge list of schools that usually involves a bunch of long shots and one good bet they don't even like. "If that good bet were the only school you got into, how would you feel?" we ask. "Bad, I guess," the student usually says. "Then don't apply," we answer. Of course, we also say, "Now, let's come up with a list that speaks more to who you are." Initially, the students think we're telling them they're not good enough or smart enough when we eliminate all but three of their long shots. "You don't think I can get into Shiny Happy U?" they'll ask, voices aquiver. "Yes and no," we answer. "You might be admitted, but we want to increase your chances at other places that might offer you what you're looking for, who might see you as a good match for them."

We're always happy with the student who has such a good list that, at the end of the season, she's been accepted by a long shot and a good bet, too, and then has a tough time deciding. The "good bet" is just as intriguing to her as the long shot. We're happy with this student because she *gets* it. **She *gets* that just because a school is easier to get into, "less selective" in the jargon, this doesn't mean it has less educational value.** Every now and then, a student of ours will buck the trend and even choose the good bet over the long shot. Of course, this will cause a flurry of buzz around the student body for several days. "How could she?" classmates will ask. "She turned down Bad-Ass College for Rinky-Dink U. What was she thinking?" She was thinking exactly what she should have been thinking: Bad-Ass College, as great a place as it might be for some, was not the best match for her. Period.

On the flip side, we've seen students accepted by their long shots and not their good bets. This happens when a good bet is made to feel like . . . well, a good bet. Just like in the dating game, when a partner feels undervalued, that person will only take so much before saying, "Oh, so you're not interested in me? Well, I'm not interested in you, either." **For many of the smaller schools, expressed interest is key, and if you've made no movement towards contacting, visiting, or communicating with the school, they'll take that sin of omission into account. Why should a college offer admission to a student who doesn't seem really interested in attending?**

Once, while visiting the admission office of a well-known school in the northeast, Eric watched as an admission rep read off a student's impressive GPA and SAT scores. "Wow," another said. "What's the problem?" "No visit," the first rep said. "Where does she live?" "Three hours away." And with that, the application, with all its impressive numbers and carefully-filled out activities list, found itself unceremoniously dropped onto the "reject" pile.

We'll talk more about visits later—and, indeed, a visit can help fine-tune the list if you're having doubts—but if you don't have the time or the means to actually go to the campus, there are other ways to establish contact with a school: meeting the admission rep who visits your town, arranging an alumni interview, or even chatting online.

Several years ago, a student, Gwenevere, was having a hard time figuring out which schools would be right for her own list. Eventually, she came up with a range—based on an organizational chart she devised—that was so well thought-out that she was accepted by all but two. In the spring, Gwenevere had a tough time deciding because she genuinely liked all of the schools, but her problem was a pretty nice one to have!

Gwenevere's chart was simple. This is what it looked like:

| College name | SAT critical reading range | SAT math range | SAT writing range | ACT range | GPA range | % accepted | Good bet Target Long shot |
|---|---|---|---|---|---|---|---|
| Colorado College | | | | | | | |
| Trinity University | | | | | | | |
| Whittier | | | | | | | |
| Kenyon | | | | | | | |
| Whitman | | | | | | | |
| Guilford | | | | | | | |
| Lake Forest | | | | | | | |
| Wash. U. | | | | | | | |
| Tulane | | | | | | | |

And that was it. By checking these basic facts and taking her own grades and scores into account, she was able to cull from the schools she knew were potential matches and make a list that was both reasonable and realistic in terms of chances of admission.

Simply, a good list will help you find that right match, but this match, as in dating, shouldn't necessarily be viewed as the end-all, be-all, answer to your dreams (because that's a tough bill to fill), but rather a place where you'll be challenged, certainly, but comfortable, too.

Some of our students take "match" to mean that they do everything in their power to convince their favorite college that they're right. While the dating analogy is obvious, students struggle with the college side of it. The advice, however, is the same: don't force the relationship to happen just because YOU think it's meant to be. After all, if you genuinely connect with someone and they you, it'll work.

"But why isn't it a match?" students will ask. "Starfleet Academy is my *favorite* school in the *entire* universe."

"That's great," we tell them, "but it's on Earth, light years away, and being close to your family is a big factor for you. You like open space, while the Academy is in the middle of a city. And you also don't like flying, right? Well, the Academy is all about space ships. Last, but just as importantly, *you hate spandex uniforms.*"

The glamour of Starfleet Academy—it is, after all, shiny and futuristic—made them mistake image for match. A friend of Eric's, upon seeing a beautiful woman walk by, commented, "*That's* my perfect woman." Was she pretty? Yes. Was she likely to be the right match? Doubtful.

**An important point to note here, too, is that colleges don't necessarily need or want a well-rounded student.** Some young scholars today think that if they do every activity under the sun, they'll be the perfect candidate. Not so much. As we'll talk about later, colleges typically want a "spiky" student, someone with some interesting characteristics that make him or her stand out. We've sat in on admission committees that have taken closer looks at students because they were from Wyoming, loved to cook, were committed to their synagogue, or wrote poetry all the time. Just as you want that match, so, too, does the college want an interesting and varied class, one that'll graduate and make the school look eclectic, thoughtful, and successful. People who pursue their passions—there's that word again—are people who tend to do great things later. Maybe you *are* a great student, basketball player, and charitable soul; the admission office will likely be impressed. They still, however, may not see you as fitting in with the rest of the freshman class.

To continue figuring out what colleges are a good "match" for you, here are a few questions you can start asking yourself: (Later, we'll talk more about the whole "getting in" thing.)

## THE LIST CHECK-LIST

### 1) Are you a country boy or city girl?

Many times, students will say they want an urban environment but then turn around and declare Dartmouth or Middlebury as their top choice—suggesting that setting really may not be a big deal. But sometimes, a student will come along who really and truly does have a strong preference and knows exactly what she wants in terms of a setting. For some, college is still college: even rural schools have a variety of cultural activities and speakers, and even institutions in bustling urban centers will still have you reading your Econ 101 textbook on a Thursday night. If you think you want *rural* or *urban*, however, make sure you have a sense of what either means. We have students apply to NYU because they like *Sex and the City*, go for a visit, and feel overwhelmed just by the tour. Weather, similarly, is also important. While you'll still be studying and inside no matter where you are, if you know you can't stand gray weather, it's better to figure this out now. Being in Colorado, our students are so accustomed to sunny skies that the cloudy winters in the northeast often prove tougher to endure than they'd anticipated.

One of Lynda's advisees came back to visit a couple of years after graduation from Kent Denver, remarking on how much she enjoyed attending college in the Washington D.C. area. She loved the political buzz, the great restaurants, and the convenient public transportation; in sum, she was one of those who had understood why she wanted to attend a college in a city. Then, counseling her counselor, she said, "Remember, college students only spend about sixteen hours a week in class. The rest of the time, they're interacting with their campus and its setting, so location really can make a huge difference!"

### 2) How do you compare big versus small and public versus private?

For the most part, we use "big" here to refer to public institutions and "small" to private—even though there are obvious exceptions. Also, as one might imagine, there are pros and cons to each category. At big public schools, you'll generally find a greater variety of classes to choose from, more social options, a lower overall cost, and quite frankly, bigger parties. However, at a big school, you might also feel like a number; you'll have to work harder to get your professors to notice you; and you'll have more competition if you want any leadership roles. At a small school, you'll typically have more face time with professors; you might find it easier to get involved in clubs and activities; you'll generally find it less difficult to get your hands on scholarship money; and you'll often feel that you're part of an intimate community. On the other hand, some people find small schools too claustrophobic, both socially and academically. Before making a decision about small or large, consider this: either could be great for your future success. As we mentioned before, some small colleges are known to prepare students exceedingly well for grad school and beyond because they allow students to develop easy working relationships with professors who will, after all, write their recommendations. However, if a student has the wherewithal to do well in a big state school, it means he has the motivation to avoid becoming just another body in a lecture hall. Because we work at a small independent school, many of our students say they're looking for the broader horizons a big university can provide, and that's fine, but once we probe a little, they're not always so sure. Sometimes all they want is a bigger place than the 400-student size of our high school. Big universities truly can provide fantastic experiences for the motivated, savvy student, but we just want to make certain everyone is informed. Here are a few common myths we'd like to expose.

- **Myth #1: You'll make more friends at big schools because of the larger population.** A number of students have reported back that the opposite is true. Though they're seeing more students each day, because of the larger groups involved in classes and clubs, making friends often requires more effort. Besides, whether you're at a school with 1,000 or 30,000, you'll still likely have the same number of real friends.

- **Myth #2: Big schools provide more courses, which is always important.** First, many small colleges have consortia with other colleges. So if you can't find the class you want at one, you can track it down at another. Also, unless you know you want to major in some exotic specialty like decoding Mayan stelae, most of the basic majors do the trick. Even if you think you want to be a journalist and Small School X doesn't have a journalism major, that doesn't really matter because most future journalists major in English or communications anyway.

- **Myth #3: There's more stuff going on.** Okay, this one may be true, but at a small college where campus life is the center of the school's culture, percentage-wise (figure a ratio of events to students), there may actually be more in the way of speakers, concerts, film festivals, and yes, even parties.

  *As an interesting side note to the "big public" versus "small private," consider this: there's a de facto affirmative action going on for boys at many small, private colleges.* Though we consider ourselves advanced in this day and age, many people still fall into traditional stereotypes: families don't mind the thought of their sons going to big state schools, but they'd often still rather have their daughter at the "cozy," smaller institutions. As a result, if you're a boy even considering some of the small colleges—such as those mentioned in Pope's *Colleges That Change Lives*—you automatically have a bit of a leg up (sorry, girls).

### 3) What's your take on the Ivies?

Again, it's not where you go but what you do once there that matters. "Ivies," the term some people use for the most "selective" colleges, are perfect fits for some but not for all. A student named Rhett, back for a visit from an Ivy he was currently attending, told Eric he hadn't been thrilled with the experience because he didn't feel that the place had been a good match. Eric had talked about this with Rhett before he decided to go, and at the time, he'd said that he was choosing the Ivy because it would open up more career options for him. Knowing he had just gotten a job offer at a hot-shot investment bank, Eric tried to be positive: "See? It worked out. You landed the job you were hoping for." "I know," Rhett said, studying his hands. "But so did a hundred other college seniors, most of whom attended colleges I'd never even heard of. And they probably had more fun than I did these past four years." Hmmm . . .

### 4) What majors interest you?

Having a sense of possible majors is important, but it by no means should be what makes or breaks your decision. If, for example, you really like a certain college, but you don't think you'll go because it doesn't have a business major, don't let that deter you. Once, a mother and CEO here in Denver called and asked Eric to tell her daughter

NOT to choose schools based on business majors. "Will you please tell her to study whatever she wants?" this mother asked. "We need people who can think and write clearly. She'll get the business experience she needs on the job, and, if she wants, she can get her MBA later." Similarly, most of Eric's philosophy-major friends from college are now higher-ups in computer companies, so go figure. The point is, use the list of majors, but keep an open mind.

### 5) What sorts of activities do you like?

If you know you want to study abroad, then begin your list by researching the schools that get ranked for having the best study-abroad programs. If attending football games is a big deal to you, make sure it's a big deal to the school. This stuff seems like a no-brainer, but it can get forgotten in the confusion. An especially thoughtful student of Lynda's stated right at the beginning of the process that she wanted a college where she could snowboard every weekend, and that was at the center of criteria for her list. The girl ended up finding a great fit in the Pacific Northwest.

### 6) What sort of political climate do you prefer?

Some students long for bohemian tie-dye-wearers who protest a new social injustice each week, while others prefer hanging out with the Young Republicans, wearing Polo shirts with creased khakis, and discussing the greatness of Barry Goldwater. Either way, while college should be a time for meeting people unlike yourself, you don't want to feel isolated, either. Think about where you fall on the political spectrum—or if it's even on your radar.

### 7) How nerdy do you like your peers?

Maybe you like being surrounded by smarties, or perhaps you prefer yucking it up with the jocks, and who knows? Maybe you like smart jocks. The intellectual climate matters.

### 8) How hard is it to travel back and forth?

Many students like the thought of being out of state, but suddenly, when faced with the reality of multiple airport transfers just to get home, they seem less sure. How important is this issue to you (and your parents)?

### 9) How much rah-rah spirit do you need?

For some, big sporting events and pep rallies are a vital part of the college experience. Others prefer a community of individuals who reject the mob in any shape or form.

### 10) How do you feel about the Greeks?

No, we're not talking about Aristotle but fraternities and sororities. Many colleges have them, and though hardly any school will admit that fraternities dominate the social scene, at some places, they really do. Maybe you like the thought of being a part of such a social club, or maybe you don't. At some schools, fraternities and sororities can be a vital, even essential part of the social experience, while at others, they can have an absolutely stagnating effect. There are even a number of schools that refuse to allow fraternities, so watch *Animal House* and decide for yourself.

### 11) Have you considered any learning differences you may have?

Many brilliant, brilliantly successful people have different learning styles. Actually, if you really think about it, everyone learns differently on some level. If, however, you are a person for whom these unique styles pose serious challenges, you'll want to look for a school with support systems. Some students receive help from parents and tutors while in high school, but then make it to college and founder because the support is gone. It's better to evaluate yourself and see where your strengths and weaknesses are before applying. More than any SAT score, this self knowledge will take you far in life.

### 12) How aware of safety issues are you?

We'd like to think of colleges as idyllic enclaves where nothing bad ever happens, but the fact of the matter is they're microcosms of the larger world. Ironically, some cozy little colleges suffer the occasional horrific crime because everyone has been lulled into a false sense of security, and some urban schools in tough neighborhoods teach their students such street smarts that the kids rarely fall victim. To find out more, go to www.ope.ed.gov/security/Search.asp, where you'll be able to compare crime rates. You can learn a lot if you visit the campus by talking to students and asking questions of the admission folks. Years ago, an NYU admission officer impressed Lynda when she asked what she could tell her students back in Colorado about staying safe in the Big Apple. He was ready for her. Taking a page of statistics from a folder, he showed her that NYU students were among the safest in the country because they were trained to be aware of their surroundings and be careful.

### 13) Would you like to spend all four years abroad?

Think you might want to jet-set to some far-off locale and study there? It'd certainly make coming home to do your laundry more of a challenge, but there are some great advantages, too—with being able to hear lots of cool accents at the top of that list. Before you apply abroad, realize that most European universities follow a different educational model with less time to explore different disciplines and electives. If this doesn't bother you, www.aucc.ca is the website of the Association of Universities and Colleges of Canada. So if "BC" means "British Columbia" to you rather than "Boston College," check it out. Also, you can order a free copy of *Canadian Universities: A Fact-Filled Guide for International Students* by calling (613) 563-1236. A former student of Eric's went to the University of British Columbia in the beautiful city of Vancouver, where she continued her study of acting. Beyond the fact that she felt sort of cool being the "international" student, she said she had a pretty traditional college sort of experience. If England is more your thing, you'll want to go to the individual university's actual website for info, but most are fairly similar in process to U.S. colleges. Beyond checking out the sites for Oxford, Cambridge, Ultrecht, or St. Andrews, there's a centralized form to apply to more than one: Britain's www.ucas.com , or Ireland's www.cao.ie. If you still need more information, www.studyintheuk.org is good, as is www.studyinaustralia.gov.au.

### 14) Do you want to be around people different from you?

Students will often say they want "diversity," which is sort of a magic word in academia. True diversity, of course, will best be reflected in a big state school or community college (Don't roll your eyes, by the way. If you look at the *USA Today's* All-USA Community College Academic Team, you won't be able to tell the difference between those kids and the best students anywhere else . . .). Even still, there are degrees of diversity just about everywhere. Beyond the color of skin, which is what most think of when talking about diversity, there's also socioeconomic, religious, and even learning style. Most students say they want diversity, but then those same students might feel uncomfortable when confronted with people too different. Do opposites attract? Not all the time.

### 15) Any thoughts about the military?

Even though we live in a time in which the military is constantly being deployed—and therefore not as attractive an option to some—the service academies are worth considering if you genuinely like the idea of serving your country. There's a catch, though: you have to *really* want to serve. A former student of Eric's got through her application, the DODMERB (the Department of Defense Medical Review Board), and even the Candidate Fitness Test, but then, after all that, she appeared at Eric's door and said, "I'm not applying." After much consideration, she decided that the only reason she had been interested in the Air Force Academy in the first place was because it provided one way for her to become an astronaut. The appeal of the going to war thing? Not so much. This seems like a common-sense sort of point, but, while the rewards of a military academy can be tremendous, the sacrifices are also; late-night pizza parties, lazy Frisbee days on the quad, and sleeping in are not exactly options. Also, you're indebted to the U.S. Government afterwards—to the tune of what usually amounts to five years in the military and three more in the reserves (to say nothing of the chance that you could die fighting in a far-off land).

The positive aspects include a free education; the fact that you become an officer upon graduation (and perhaps even a gentleman/woman); hands-on, cutting edge experience for future jobs in engineering, computers, and aviation, among others; immediate, real-world experiences; and vague as it might sound to some, there's also the notion that you're sacrificing yourself for a greater cause—not something to be taken lightly.

What do you have to do if you're interested? Before anything, check out one of the websites: Navy: www.usna.edu; Air Force: www.usafa.af.mil; Army: www.usma.edu; Coast Guard: www.cga.edu; and Merchant Marine: www.usmma.edu.

From there, you'll want to make sure the basic requirements are met. These include: 1) being between 17-22 years old and an unmarried U.S.

citizen who's not responsible for any children; 2) a strong high school record (which includes four years each of English and math, three to four years of lab science—depending on whether you're going into the Air Force Academy or not—and strong teacher recommendations); 3) leadership ability as seen in school and community activities; 4) good physical health—which usually excludes asthma, color blindness, eating disorders, and even some learning differences—and above-average strength.

What's the timeline? In the spring of junior year, once you've decided that you meet the basic requirements, you can start a file at the academy of your choice. The summer after junior year, you should get started on your medical requirements, and just as importantly, you'll need to apply for a nomination from your representative, two senators, or even the Vice President. In case you're curious, you're allowed to try for four nominations, so that's how many you should go for. Also, know that those with a high enough "whole candidate score" can by-pass the nomination. This score is 60% academic, 30% leadership, and 10% fitness. In senior year, you need to make sure you have that nomination in hand and that you've finished your testing. You might want to fit in one more visit just to make sure a military academy is for you. (While you're there, ask one of the freshmen "plebes" how his or her experience is going. If you're still convinced, a service academy is definitely where you belong!)

By the way, guys, just because you might have heard that some women like the look of a guy in uniform, that alone doesn't constitute reason to join!

### 16) How strongly do you feel about art?

We encourage everyone to take art classes at some point in their lives, but if you're the sort of student whose main motivation for coming to school in the first place is your drawing or photo class, then you might want to consider seriously an art college. We've had students who practically had to force themselves to apply to "regular" colleges until we pointed out some of these wonderful art institutions, at which point they lit up—realizing for the first time, perhaps, that college didn't have to be four more years of what to them seemed like traditional academic drudgery.

By the way, gone are the days when an art major is seen as something frivolous (or gone *should* be the days, at least). Art grads are involved in fashion, auto design, video game development, special effects for movies, magazine illustration, and even toy design, to name a few possible careers. While you can certainly pursue your creative dreams, an art degree will also appeal to that business-minded uncle of yours, too.

Just so you know, many traditional colleges provide wonderful arts programs, so if you want to make sure you're receiving that broad liberal arts education, then consider this route. These schools range from the big-name Brown to the lesser-known (but excellent) Muhlenberg College. For a comprehensive list, see *Creative Colleges: A Guide for Student Actors, Artists, Dancers, Musicians and Writers*, which has profiles of 200 programs as well as tips from admission officers and students. Also see *Rugg's Recommendations on the Colleges*, one of the books we mentioned in the previous chapter.

If you're already focused and ready to get down to the business of making serious art, then you might want to consider an actual art college. A few names we hear time and again include (but are not limited to): RISD (Rhode Island School of Art and Design), a highly selective school with fantastic programs in painting and illustration; MICA (Maryland Institute College of Art), another selective art school that even boasts a major in environmental design; New Hampshire Institute of Art, a small, user-friendly campus with a student body that adores the place; Tyler School of Art (Temple University), a less expensive state school definitely worth checking out; Columbia College Chicago, a big art school with a wide range of respected programs; Ringling School of Art and Design, an institution that provides outstanding classes in animation and illustration; and Memphis College of Art, a small, private college with a supportive atmosphere.

When looking at art colleges, be aware of some of the for-profit institutions out there. Some art teachers are under the impression that these schools are after the students' money more than anything else. You can certainly get a good education at some of these places, but just visit with your eyes open.

Once you've decided you want to pursue *something* in the arts, along with the application, you'll also need to prepare a portfolio. Most art colleges provide portfolio critiques during the National Portfolio Days held in various locations around the country, and we'd strongly encourage you to take advantage of this chance to have an insider review your work. (To make sure the schools you want to visit will be in attendance, check out www.portfolioday.net.)

A few tips to make your portfolio day run more smoothly:

1) Seek a second opinion. You might find that one reviewer doesn't like your portfolio at all, but then the next one thinks it's the best thing since sliced bread.

2) Put your insecurities aside. Remember, the reviewers want to help you, and since they don't have much time, they might come off as a little rushed or short. Take into account what they say, and try not to take any constructive criticism too personally.

3) Make notes on the reviewers' comments after each session is over.

4) Limit your portfolio to between fifteen and twenty pieces of your best (and probably most recent) work. Also, make sure that a healthy number of these are observational drawings.

5) Think about using a presentation case. It'll cost a little more, but it'll make your work stand out. (And whatever case you use, make sure it's marked clearly with your name, phone number, and something that'll make it easy to spot from among all the other portfolios.)

6) Cash in on that favor a friend owes you and ask for a "line-sitter." As lines can be long, you might want to have someone wait in one line for you while you wait in another. (This is where cell phones come in handy.)

7) Do your homework. Read about the reviewer you'll be meeting as well as the college itself.

8) Arrive early.

9) Avoid bringing in big, clunky pieces. For sculptures, you'll need good photos showing more than one angle.

10) Check with your art teacher before going. He or she will be able to tell you how best to order your work (in other words, which pieces are the strongest), as well as offer general tips and confidence-builders.

11) Investigate the college with the short line. While everyone else is waiting to talk to RISD, you might have a serendipitous moment and discover a hidden gem!

## MAKING LISTS—THREE CASE STUDIES

Let's consider three hypothetical candidates and make short sample lists for each of them. First, we need to remove some of the "wild cards" that could invalidate the logic of our otherwise very realistic lists. Remember, we go into the list-making process objectively with eyes wide open!

Let's assume that none of our candidates has any special edge—we have nobody whose mother just funded a new particle accelerator for a college's physics department, nobody is a student of color, nobody is a recruited Division I athlete, nobody's mother or father attended one of the schools under consideration, nobody just won the Nobel Prize, nobody is applying ED, nobody has a heart-rending story of living in a car while supporting an invalid parent and six siblings, and nobody has ever been in serious trouble. All have written decent essays, attend a high school with a solid reputation, and have compiled a respectable list of activities. In sum, let's assume a reasonably level playing field in terms of background.

We're looking mainly at SAT Critical Reading (CR) and Math (M) mid-50% range of scores here because they give a quick indication of what a college is looking for in terms of academic qualifications. We've used the terms you've seen before:

- "Good bet" (You have an 80%-90% chance of getting in.)

- "Target" (The odds are 50-50; say you have a 40%-60% chance.)

- "Long shot" (These schools are so selective and arbitrary that it's virtually impossible to predict who'll be admitted; we can call this a 10% or less chance of admission.)

**Barbie Bionic**—Barbie has her heart set on a small, selective liberal arts school. She'd prefer New England, but she's open to other geographical areas. What matters to her is good teaching, small classes, and a setting conducive to academic growth in a congenial atmosphere. Her SAT's are impressive, with a 700 on Critical Reading and 690 Math;

her GPA is 3.85; and she has four AP courses on her record. On the two AP exams she took last year, she earned a 4 and a 5, and she's taking two more AP's in her senior year. Her recommendations characterize her as "a delight to teach." Here are some colleges she might reasonably include on her list:

*Williams College: CR 650-760, M 650-740*
For Barbie, an application to Williams makes sense because it fits her main criteria and because she's a strong candidate. We might call it a "target," but there's a caveat—it's a very selective place, and while her scores definitely put her in the running, there's a "long-shot" feel.

*Smith College: CR 590-710, M 560-670*
Barbie can definitely place Smith in the "target" category, and it's looking like it's close to a good bet.

*Carleton College: CR 670-750, M 660-740*
Again, Barbie is definitely in the running here, and we can call it a "target" but not sure thing by any means.

*Whitman College: CR 610-720, M 620-700*
This is another good "target" for Barbie.

*Scripps College: CR 650-740, M 630-700*
Yep, another "target."

Counselor Commentary: You can see that a student like Barbie, bright and accomplished, has the qualifications for the kind of school she'd like to attend. A tough thing about these fine, small liberal arts colleges is that they just don't admit very many kids, so while good grades and scores put her in the running, there aren't a lot of assurances. Also, the fact that she's female makes it just a wee bit more challenging. Simply, she has a lot of strong female competition out there. We'd probably advise her to make a slightly longer list than most, say eight to ten schools. Here are some "good bets" for her to consider:

*Hendrix College: CR 560-690, M 590-660*
Barbie's favorite grandmother lives in Arkansas, and she also loves all things outdoorsy—two factors that pushed her to consider a school outside the northeast. Though Hendrix is certainly

selective, if Barbie shows sincere interest, she might just be able to fit it into her "good bet" category.

*Roger Williams University: CR 500-590, M 520-600*
Barbie has toyed with the idea of studying architecture, and the fact that Roger Williams has a good program along with a solid liberal arts line-up piqued her interest. (The fact that it's in a beautiful setting doesn't hurt, either!)

*Franklin and Marshall College: CR 580-670, M 600-690*
With a best friend at Franklin and Marshall, Barbie has heard it's a good place. This one should be somewhere hovering between a "target" and a "good bet" for her, if she plays her cards right.

**Dudley Dutiful**—Dudley is looking for a medium-sized school where he can enjoy an active Greek-centered social life in a setting with enthusiastic school spirit. He has earned respectable scores: CR 620, M 650, and his GPA of 3.3 indicate he's a hardworking student. Last year he took an AP exam, which he passed with a 4, and this year, as a senior he's taking two more AP's. Dudley's recommendations term him "an all-around great kid." Here are some colleges he might reasonably consider:

*Bucknell University: CR 630-720, M 660-740*
Dudley's scores fall below the mid 50% range in both categories, so we'd better call Bucknell a "long shot" for him. That doesn't mean he shouldn't apply. He loves this great school!

*Boston College: CR 610-700, M 640-720*
Let's call BC a "target" for Dudley, but we can't really count on admission at this ever-more-selective and very popular school.

*Miami University of Ohio: CR 540-640, M 570-660*
Miami is definitely a "target" for Dudley!

*Wake Forest: CR 610-690, M 630-710*
We'll put Wake in the same category as BC—he's in the running, but we can't count on his getting in.

*Southern Methodist University: CR 560-650, M 580-670*
SMU would be a great spot for Dudley, and we're lucky we can put it in the "good bet" category!

Counselor Commentary: Dudley will do ok in the process because he has great schools on his list. In addition, we think he should apply to his state university, too, because he'll find the Greek life and the school spirit that appeal to him, along with a wide array of courses.

**Leonora Laidback**—Leonora's top consideration is a warm climate; she wants good academics in a cheerful setting. She also likes service work. Her SAT's are CR 520 and M 510, her GPA is 2.8, and there are no AP courses on her transcript. Her recommendations describe her as "a lovely girl who is a good friend to her classmates." Here are some schools she might put on her list:

*Whittier College: CR 480-590, M 480-590*
Whittier would be a fine target for Leonora; they have great programs in sunny Southern California.

*Flagler College: CR 520-610, M 510-590*
Flagler in Florida—a good target, too!

*New Mexico State: CR 420-550, M 430-560*
New Mexico would welcome Leonora, and she should put NMSU in her "good bet" category.

*Loyola (New Orleans): CR 560-690, M 540-650*
Loyola is a long-shot with Leonora's scores, but she loves New Orleans, and she can put it on her list.

*Occidental: CR 590-690, M 600-690*
Oxy is even more of a long shot.

Counselor Commentary: Because climate is so important to her, Leonora may want to think about adding Arizona State and the University of Arizona to her list. They're bigger than the others, but they have warm weather and good course offerings.

As a parting note, let's consider the extremes of the spectrum: Stan Superstar and Stuart Slacker. Even the top kids can't always write their own ticket, and even the ones who barely graduate can go to college! Here's the deal: Stan, applying to Harvard, Yale, and Princeton is entering into that world of the super-unpredictable. Even his 4.4 GPA, six AP scores of 5, and perfect 800's on the SAT's don't ensure his admission to these places—but he'll definitely be in the running. Stuart, with his 2.1 GPA and SAT's in the 400's may need to attend his local community college for a year or two while he builds a record that will prove to a four-year college that he's indeed capable of doing the work that they'll require.

> ### A Thought About Finding Your Right Match:
>
> A University of Minnesota study recently revealed that "expression of emotion in most romantic relationships can be related back to a person's attachment experiences during earlier social development."
>
> Maybe. Either way, it's still up to you. Love means making decisions.

NOTHIN' IN MY TEETH, LOOKIN' GOOD...

**Chapter 6**

# Pre-Date Primping

## Course work, standardized tests, and EA/ED

*"Man is born to live, not to prepare for life."*
—BORIS PASTERNAK

So you've done your research; you have a list of schools that seem to be potentially good fits; and now it's time for a few housekeeping items. As with dating, you want to prepare but not *over* prepare. As no one wants to be on a date with someone who's desperate, colleges don't like desperation, either. A friend once told Eric how on a date he found himself sort of liking the girl until she blurted out the fact that she hadn't been asked out in months. "At that point," he said later, "I lost interest."

Similarly, a student of ours practically attacked an admission rep who was visiting our high school campus recently, thrusting a slick, glossy portfolio that included, among other less-than-essential items, head shots. "Uh . . . thanks?" the rep said, glancing around for help.

So here are the basics to make sure you're ready to go:

## COURSES

Colleges want to see "all major food groups" represented: math, science, English, history, and language. They want to see that you're challenging yourself by taking some of the toughest courses ("rigor" is a word that comes up often in admission offices), and that there are no gaps in your education. Fairly often, we'll have a student who wants to drop a language class so that he can take an extra science—or vice versa. We typically assure Joey Student that there's no need to start thinking about majors in high school and that it's best not to drop anything. Every now and again, however, ol' Joey will convince us that he's so passionate about a subject he can't *not* take the class. In this case, we encourage him to assure whatever admission rep he talks to that he's not running *from* one subject but rather *to* another. Even so, we remind him that he's leaving a gap on his transcript. ***Also, consider this fact when thinking about how to approach your classes: many colleges consider the fall semester of your senior year the best indicator of how well you'll do in college.*** The point is, if there's a time in your life to buckle down and do well in school, that's it.

## STANDARDIZED TESTS

As we mentioned before, there are schools that don't require scores. If your numbers are high, you should send them anyway because this will show your strength in yet one more area, and high scores make the college's average applicant numbers look higher—which makes everyone happy. There are some state schools, such as the ones in Arizona, that have an "or . . . or . . . or" set-up, meaning that you could have a certain SAT score OR a certain GPA OR a certain ACT. As for deciding between SAT and ACT, that's up to you. Most of our students who take both end up with similar scores. Those who do better on the ACT tend to be strong, speedy readers, who appreciate the no-penalty-for-guessing (and hence, less gamesmanship) aspect. So, if this sounds like you, it's a test worth considering.

**A few facts to help you decide between the ACT and the SAT.**

1) The SAT lasts three hours, 45 minutes while the ACT a mere two hours, 55 minutes (unless you take the optional writing on the ACT, which adds another 30 minutes).

2) ACT questions tend to be more information-centered and straightforward.

3) Where the SAT focuses on vocabulary, the ACT stresses grammar and syntax.

4) There's less of a gender gap between females and males on the ACT than on the SAT.

5) Bright underachiever? Think about the SAT.

6) You get ¼ point off for each wrong answer on the SAT but no points off on the ACT.

7) The SAT has no science or trigonometry, while the ACT has both.

8) The ACT has no order of difficulty, while with the SAT, the questions get progressively harder.

9) All SAT scores go to colleges if any are sent, but you can send individual ACT scores.

10) The SAT is a little trickier, the ACT more straightforward.

11) Prone to careless mistakes? It's tougher to "mis-grid" on the ACT bubble sheet for the simple reason that if question #13 has answers A through E, then #14 will be F through J.

12) Related to mistakes, if you were to challenge a question (even if it's not something that's usually worth the time spent), the SAT still charges $50 for the whole thing to be reviewed. With the ACT, one question can be challenged for free, while a hand-scored "verification" is a mere $30.

## NEW SAT & ACT SCORE COMPARISON

| ACT If you scored... | Old SAT (just critical reading and math) or a... | NEW SAT It's about the same as a... |
|---|---|---|
| 36 | 1600 | 2400 |
| 35 | 1560-1590 | 2340 |
| 34 | 1510-1550 | 2260 |
| 33 | 1460-1500 | 2190 |
| 32 | 1410-1450 | 2130 |
| 31 | 1360-1400 | 2040 |
| 30 | 1320-1350 | 1980 |
| 29 | 1280-1310 | 1920 |
| 28 | 1240-1270 | 1860 |
| 27 | 1210-1230 | 1820 |
| 26 | 1170-1200 | 1760 |
| 25 | 1130-1160 | 1700 |
| 24 | 1090-1120 | 1650 |
| 23 | 1060-1080 | 1590 |
| 22 | 1020-1050 | 1530 |
| 21 | 980-1010 | 1500 |
| 20 | 940-970 | 1410 |
| 19 | 900-930 | 1350 |
| 18 | 860-890 | 1290 |
| 17 | 810-850 | 1210 |
| 16 | 760-800 | 1140 |
| 15 | 710-750 | 1060 |
| 14 | 660-700 | 1000 |
| 13 | 590-650 | 900 |
| 12 | 520-580 | 780 |
| 11 | 500-510 | 750 |

Source: http://www.collegeboard.com

## HOW OFTEN TO TAKE THE TESTS

Now, as to how often you should take these fun-filled, action-packed tests, we'd recommend at least twice. Typically, scores go up the second time around just because students feel more comfortable by then—as comfortable, that is, as one can be filling out bubble sheets for almost four hours! When you consider a retake, think about the following:

1) The College Board puts all scores into a "score bank" so that any time you send any test results to a college, all the previous test scores go along—except PSAT scores and AP scores. Just so you know. In other words, if you're re-taking an SAT or an SAT Subject Test, make sure your heart is in it, and do your best work because colleges will see the results. Caveat: Lynda has known students who have done one last testing in, say, December of the senior year and **not** have it sent to a college. In other words, these kids have already sent off their previous test results but want to see if one more go at the Subject Test in Tasmanian Folk Music would raise their score by 20 points. If the muses were guiding the bubbling that day, then the students send the score after seeing it.

2) On the other hand, ACT allows you to send any one set of scores from any one testing. A college will only see the testing(s) that you designate. So if you think you might read a little faster next time, you have nothing to lose except a few $ and a Saturday morning.

3) Do you have reason to think you'll do better? Are you just assuming that "test early, test often" makes sense? (Lynda actually heard a college rep say this to a group of students one time . . . go figure!) Or, did you just work your way through a book of ten real SAT's, scoring each exam and figuring out what you did wrong and what you did right? Serious prep constitutes a valid reason for a re-test! On the flip side, maybe the scores on your second testing dropped. You had the flu, you just broke up with your boyfriend, you needed to go to the bathroom, you had a hangnail—in sum, there was a *reason* that you were not at your best on test day, and you know you'll be in better shape next time around.

4) SAT Subject Tests have a logic all their own. Sure, you're still doing multiple-choice, and a wrong answer hurts more than an omission, but these exams are focused on curriculum. So, for example, you'd want to take the test in U.S. history right after you finished that class. But what if, like Eric and Lynda's students, you

take the Spanish exam at the end of the A.P. Spanish *Language* Course (after all, they just studied for the A.P. exam . . .), but you go on to take the A.P. Spanish *Literature* course. Literature is reading and vocab, so if the kids aren't completely satisfied with their score at the end of the language class, it makes sense for them to have another go at the same test when they're in the lit class. And, speaking of the language Subject Tests, most have a choice of a listening component or not, with the listening version only available at a certain time (generally November). Complicated? You betcha. Have a little pow-wow with your teacher, and study the free booklet that The College Board provides. You can also buy real tests to take for practice.

5) Are you going to beat yourself up if you don't get into the school of your choice and you think it *just might be* because you opted out of taking the SAT one more time? This is a tough question to answer, and you're the only one who can do it. On the one hand, college acceptances are rarely that cut-and-dried, but on the other, this process tends to make everyone go a little nuts at times, and so you might end up blaming a rejection on any darned thing. So if you think you might be doing "woulda, coulda, shoulda" to yourself, take the test again.

## TEST PREP

SAT/ACT preparation is another decision that needs to be up to you. If you think you'd be invested in the test-prep classes, either with one of the big companies or with a private tutor, then go ahead and take them. However, if you feel that you'd be bitter, don't. The unfortunate fact of the matter is that many students today *do* prep for these tests, and there certainly are tricks that help improve scores. Until a better, fairer test is developed, we're stuck with what we have. Classes can help, but they typically end up giving less of a big boost than the ads proclaim. Consider a class if you won't make yourself sit down and take the practice tests. For such a person, the structure is invaluable.

If you are disciplined, there are some books and online sources that will help you learn plenty on your own. They range from the College Board's *The Official SAT Study Guide* to *Cracking the ACT from Princeton Review*. A few of these online prep resources are: www.number2.com, www.act.org, www.collegeboard.com, www.petersons.com, and www. princetonreview.com/college/testprep. Also, the College Board will, for a fee, send you your old test with the corrected answers to study— which could make you feel even worse, but you really *can* learn from your screw-ups if you have a mind to.

### A Few Testing Tips

While coaching for the tests is a whole industry, and we certainly wouldn't want to interfere with the economy by taking business away from any of the folks who sell advice for a living, we thought we'd offer just a few tips for standardized testing.

### SAT and ACT in General:

The shape you're in mentally and physically is every bit as important as how many hours you might have spent prepping. *Never underestimate test readiness!* Mainly, this means being wide awake and feeling your best for the test. We'd suggest:

- ✔ To get your brain in "multiple-choice mode," for two or three weeks in advance of the test day, spend about half an hour each night answering sample questions and checking answers.

- ✔ Do at least one whole sample test under timed conditions the weekend before. Score it and look at the questions you missed. Try to figure out where you went wrong. Also, look at what you did right!

- ✔ At least a week before test day, establish a sleep pattern that gets you out of bed at the same hour you'll need to be up on test day—and we don't mean 15 minutes before the test is to begin.

- ✔ A few days in advance, go find the test center; locate parking areas, bathrooms, and drinking fountains. You don't want to worry about this sort of stuff when you need to be worrying about filling in ovals.

- ✔ Eat a normal breakfast on test day. If you never eat bacon and eggs, don't start now.

- ✔ Take a snack to eat at the breaks—your brain and body will need fuel.

- ✔ Dress in layers—no telling whether the room will be chilly or suffocating.

- ✔ Go to the bathroom before the test starts, whether you need to or not. No kidding!

- ✔ Wear a watch and budget your time, but don't panic.

- ✔ FOCUS!

- ✔ We'd advise you to eschew (now *there's* a vocab word!) games-personship. You can waste a lot of time counting how many questions you've answered and figuring how many correct responses you need to get some certain score. You'd do better just to use your brain to think through each item and consider each possible response.

## SAT:

- ✔ Guess, but guess wisely. If you can narrow the choices to two for a 50-50 chance, by all means, ANSWER!

- ✔ Remember that the answer to an easy question counts just as much as the answer to a tough one. Rather than agonize for too long, skip questions that seem too hard—you can go back to them later if you have time. Mark the ones you skip in your test booklet. Be sure to also skip that number on the answer sheet. (Lynda once spent half a test erasing . . . ouch!)

### Critical Reading:

- ✔ If a reading section is too weird or boring, skip it and go on to the next one. You can always go back.

- ✔ As you practice, experiment with what works best for you—reading the questions before the passage or reading the passage first.

- ✔ Be sure to read the title and the bit in italics before you start on a passage.

- ✔ Answer questions that have line references first. Need we remind you to go to the line in question before responding?

✔ Some people like to skim the passage and have developed their own methods for doing so; others like to read every word. Practice both ways to see what works best for you.

✔ Underline key words; use circles and arrows; anything to help you make the passage your own for those few minutes you're working with it.

✔ Don't freak out if you don't know a word; nobody knows *all* those words!

## Math:

✔ You *did* charge up your calculator, right?

✔ Set up the problem in the margin of the test booklet before you touch that electronic device!

✔ Be careful with little things like plusses and minuses. The folks at ETS love to trick their clients (you) with easy-to-screw-up details.

✔ There are basically only six or seven *types* of problems, so realize that you don't have to know how to do every kind of math in the world. Just these.

## Writing:

✔ While you're mostly sweating about the essay (see the specific essay tips that follow), don't overlook the multiple-choice. One big help is to sub-vocalize (say aloud in your head) the answer you want to use before blackening that oval. Don't move your lips or the proctors might go ballistic. For the sentence completions, if you need to guess, pick the shortest choice—it's often the correct one.

## ACT:

✔ This test is more straight-forward, but it's still blackening ovals.

✔ Because there's no penalty for guessing, GUESS!

✔ There is a lot to read here. Nobody expects you to get through all of it.

✔ For the Science Reading and Reasoning section, go to the graphs and charts *first*. Answer as many questions as you can from the information you find there *before* you tackle the text.

**Writing Tips for the Essay Part of the SAT and the ACT:**

✔ Trying to write an essay in 25 minutes (SAT) or 30 (ACT) is nerve-wracking. Practice with sample topics from those prep books will help a lot. These essays are scored by teachers who have specific guidelines to use in their grading, but nobody expects you to produce a perfectly polished piece in such a short amount of time. That said, consider the following:

✔ Time is of the essence, so have your watch where you can see it. Basically, you need to spend three to five minutes understanding the question (if you don't do this first step, none of the rest will matter much) and then making a *very* brief outline to organize your response. Figure on 20-23 minutes to write. Save one to two minutes to quickly check over your masterpiece.

✔ Write neatly and clearly. Actual human beings are blasting through these essays. These folks are closed up in an uncomfortable room. Their eyes burn. Their shoulders ache. They are *longing* to pick up a legible response.

✔ In a short introduction, present a succinct, provable thesis statement that addresses the topic.

✔ Body paragraphs, two or three of them, should begin with strong topic sentences. Specific support for your points from current events, history, literature, or your own experiences should follow.

✔ Conclude, but avoid words like "clearly." If what you wrote is clear, you don't need to say that it is. By the way, your conclusion should *conclude*, not repeat.

✔ Stay on topic, even if you suddenly have some brilliant inspiration that goes in another direction.

✔ Longer is generally better.

✔ Acknowledge the other point of view, but don't get lost in it.

✔ Write in a clear, direct manner. Remember what your English teachers have taught you. A bunch of stiff prose with long words you'd not normally use will impress nobody.

**SAT Subject Tests:** If you haven't gotten your fill of tests yet, there's one more (or three more, depending on how you look at it), which would be the SAT Subject Tests. These tests are subject-specific, and you can take three in one day, if you'd like. (Or just one, if that's your preference.) Many juniors take them in June, before things get too crazy with their senior calendar. Consider taking Math I or II, depending on your level, then one or two other tests in your strongest subjects. Check the SAT Subject Tests required by the colleges you're researching. Even if the schools you're considering don't require any, we still recommend you sign up. First, your college list might change, and second, the extra info could help.

**For the day of the test: (as if you haven't heard this before)**

1) photo id

2) registration bulletin

3) several #2 pencils

4) a calculator with energized Energizers

5) a bucket of ice water to dunk your head in afterwards

## CONSIDER ED AND EA

"ED" refers to "Early Decision" and "EA" to "Early Action." Except for the few schools that do "single choice" Early Action, Early Action simply means that you can apply early and find out around December whether or not you're accepted, and you have no obligations. "Single choice" Early Action means just that—you're allowed to apply early to only one college, but you're not obligated to attend.

With Early Decision, however, if you're accepted at that college, you commit to going, and you must withdraw all your other applications. Some universities will say that an Early Decision bid can be the equivalent of 100 extra points on the SAT. However, if you're not 100%, absolutely positively sure that that college is your first choice, ED is a terrible strategy. Not long ago, a student—Eurydice, we think her name was—entered Eric's office and said, out of the blue, that she'd be applying to Brown ED. This was the first time he'd heard her even mention Brown, so he began to ask her about it.

"Are you sure?" he asked, continuing with, "I'd only recommend it if you're absolutely positive. It's not worth it otherwise."

"I'm sure," she said.

Eric, however, wasn't convinced. A week later, Eurydice came back with a panicked expression, and Eric knew what was coming. "Is there any way to take that back?" she blurted out.

"What happened?" he asked.

"It's just that I visited Wash U and immediately fell in love. That would be a much better match for me. Is there anything we can do?"

"There is one thing," Eric said. "What's that?" "Hope you don't get in." Early Decision is binding, and while you won't go to jail if you back out, you may wish you had. Many admission officers talk to one another, and not only would you be ruining that college for future applicants from your high school, but those admission folks have ways of putting the squeeze on you, too. One admission rep explained how, after a student had reneged an ED acceptance, he learned where the student had decided to go, and then required the student to write letters of apology to both institutions—each of which had withdrawn their acceptances—and explain what happened.

By the way, that extra-100-point-boost equivalent on your SAT for ED isn't going to be enough to make a real difference at the super-selective schools. There is ONE instance when you will grab a real strategic boost by using ED on a long shot—that's when you're an alumni child. Many colleges (though not all) will go out of their way to accept the offspring of alums who apply ED, that is, when the college knows that the student will definitely attend if accepted. Otherwise, if the student applies with the regular pool to mom or dad's alma mater, the admission office tends to think that the app is coming just to appease the parents. One of Lynda's advisees actually went out of his way to make sure the interviewer understood that he was applying *only* because of parental pressure. He behaved so rudely during his visit to the college that there was no way they'd have taken him!

### ED or not ED, That is the Question . . .

Are you ready for the commitment? The head of our upper school passed along this sage advice to help students figure out for themselves:

- Is the school REALLY your first choice, and ED is not something you're doing just to strategize?

- Have you visited? (More specifically, have you visited when regular classes are in session, spending the night in a dorm?)

- Have you visited similar schools to see how your choice compares?

- Are you ready to deal with the financial consequences, knowing you won't have the full spectrum of aid opportunities to choose from?

- Are you ready for a school to see your record this early in the process?

As a P.S. to all this talk of early applications, if you are accepted Early Action, DO NOT go scalp hunting. As we explained in Chapter 2, it's simply not fair. Both Eric and Lynda have seen students get into their first pick and then ride out the season "just to see" where else they'd get in. As we said, this can block other good candidates, even from your own school. Second, if you think extra acceptances will give you bragging rights as an adult, know that they won't. Adults who talk about all the colleges that accepted them are about as lame as adults who talk about their SAT scores. Finally, just as when people "trophy hunt" in relationships, seeing how many they can date at once, realize that this is a sign of insecurity.

### ROLLING

This term simply means that a college reads applications as they come in, and the admission office makes decisions as they read. In September and early October, when there are fewer apps coming in, this decision-making process generally goes much faster than it does later. Many state schools work this way, and we counsel students who are possibly interested in staying in state to get these apps done ASAP. If the college accepts you, it's just fabulous to have an early "YES!" If the admission folks decide to wait about making a decision until they can see more grades or test scores, you still haven't lost a thing, and you have already sent off your first application.

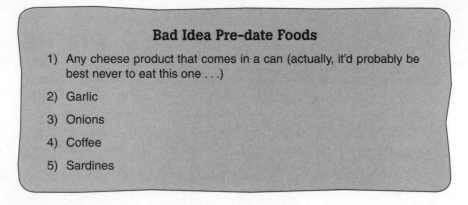

**Bad Idea Pre-date Foods**

1) Any cheese product that comes in a can (actually, it'd probably be best never to eat this one . . .)

2) Garlic

3) Onions

4) Coffee

5) Sardines

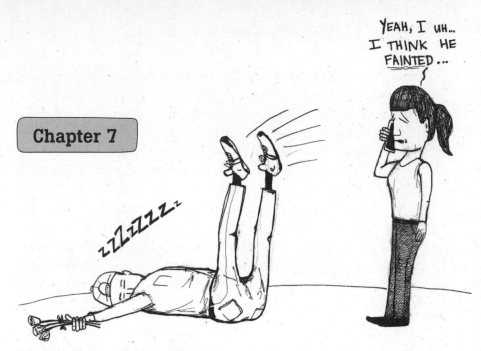

# The First Date

## The interview and visits

> *"By our first strange and fatal interview,/By all desires which thereof did ensue."*
>
> —John Donne

Until now, it's all been theory. You've been reading and talking and thinking, then reading and talking and thinking some more. Now it's time to get out and go on your first date. In college parlance, the first date is equivalent to the visit and the interviews. Ready? Buckle up, because this is where things get lively.

### THINGS TO KEEP IN MIND WHEN VISITING A COLLEGE

1) Remember that, as in the dating world, the flashy ones don't always make the best partners. Ever heard the saying, "the candle that burns brightest burns out the fastest?" It applies to those hot

romances that sizzle at the start but then fade quickly and leave you with nothing. Some visits to colleges are like that. Admission offices know how to wow kids, showing off their new gym with the climbing wall, their state-of-the-art science center, and we can't forget, those super cool-campus apartments that only up-per classmen end up in anyway. There are many eye-boggling things going on in schools nowadays, and while most of these universities are fantastic on some level, don't let the razzmatazz make you think they're all perfect for you. "What did you like about the school?" we've asked students upon their return from a college visit. "I don't know . . . it was just . . . awesome," they'll say. Hmmm . . . maybe it would be a good idea to focus on some specifics.

2) Go with your gut, but be aware that it is, after all, just your gut. We're firm believers in the power of intuition and what your in-stincts tell you. However, sometimes the famous "gut" is more fickle than anyone would like to admit. A student returned from a visit to Duke University one summer, previously his top choice, and told Eric he wouldn't be applying. "Why not?" Eric asked. After a little prying, the student said that a dairy truck had turned over and a good portion of the campus had, as a result, ended up smelling like rancid milk. "Is that it?" asked Eric.

"Oh . . . it was really quiet, too," the boy said.

Other students have been turned off by schools because they didn't see any "hot" girls. Or the tour guide had bed-head. Or someone chucked a keg out of a window—which, to be honest, was likely pretty entertaining. Now, any of these things could end up being important factors in your decision, but just be aware of what exactly influences you. If, after much thought, you realize that the only reason you didn't like Hallelujah U was because the tour guide tripped while walking backward, remember that you'll probably never see that tour guide again.

3) Consider the time of year when you go. Summers are slow and often boring, so it's usually tougher to imagine yourself on a cam-pus when all you see are middle-school kids there for a sports camp running around the quad. In the summer, however, you can

often get a little more interaction with someone in the admission office because it's the one time of year the office slows down. Fall of your senior year is good for visits, but it's tougher for everyone's schedule. You won't be able to take much time off then, and admission offices are over-booked. Spring of senior year also works, but such a visit would only serve to satisfy any lingering questions you might have about a place, and you wouldn't get credit during the actual admission process for your visit (more about this later when we talk about staying in touch).

4) DO NOT FALL IN LOVE WITH JUST ONE COLLEGE. Play the field! Orpheus, a former student of Lynda's, told her early in his *junior* year that he loved nowhere else as much as Pomona. It was the only school for him, the end-all, be-all of the universe. The sun rose and set over Pomona's campus. Lynda's first concern with poor, Pomona-obsessed Orpheus was that, if he didn't get in, he'd feel absolutely crushed. Her second concern was that if he did get in, there was no way it could ever meet his expectations. The latter ended up happening, and after the first semester, Orpheus called Lynda to talk about transferring. A very social guy, Orpheus was bummed by the fact that most students studied every weeknight. She talked with him about expectations when he came back to Colorado for a visit a few weeks later. As a result, he decided to stick it out a little longer. When all was said and done, he ended up staying all four years and really enjoying the rest of his time there—and even becoming a more serious student in the process! The moral: don't get too serious too fast; things don't always turn out as well as they did for Orpheus. (Now, if you can't see the dating analogy here . . .)

5) See about staying overnight when you visit. The college might have a former student from your high school there who'll host you. Either way, the admission office will likely be glad to set you up with someone. The occasional horror story does emerge from such a visit (with a drunken host throwing up in the visitor's shoes topping our list), but in general, it's the best way to get a sense of the place.

6) Attend a class or two. One former student absolutely loved a school on paper. The tour guide was great, and the admission

office helpful. But then she went to an upper-level film class and found the students apathetic and uninterested. The professor asked basic questions that seemed way too easy even to her, so she felt her zeal begin to wane. Another student visited a physics class at a high-powered university. Unfortunately, our girl was the only one listening to the prof; the rest of the class seemed to be reading the newspaper, dozing, or chatting among themselves. Certainly when visiting a class, you won't ever know what you'll find. It could be a Friday morning, in which case the kids will look like extras from a zombie movie, and you won't find the scintillating exchange you might have been hoping for. Even still, visiting a class or talking with a professor can reveal plenty.

7) While on a tour—or afterwards, if you're scared of looking like a dork—take notes. Write down big things and little things, anything that will help you remember the place in a more personal way than view books and websites can. Later, you'll be thankful you did, as most of the schools will blur at least somewhat in your memory.

8) On a visit, chat with students. Don't be afraid to grab a few (they're easy to nab as they come out of their holes in the morning). Then explain you're a visiting high school student and that you're thinking about attending their glorious institution. Pure and simple, ask what they like about the place. One or two questions will generally be sufficient, but make sure the student doesn't seem to be in a rush. Don't be embarrassed about doing this. First, if anyone is ever rude—and no one is—then that speaks poorly of the school, not you. Second, your asking is infinitely better than your nerd-o mom tweaking out and saying something embarrassing, right? One of Eric's own secrets is that he often approaches the dudeliest, most Neanderthal-looking guy, and if HE ends up being polite and articulate—which, almost every time, he has been—then that's a good sign.

9) When talking with either students or the tour guide, ask the questions that matter. College folks are ready for your bland, pointless questions. They're just waiting for your "what's the social life here like?" with a smirk, and they're about to pounce on your "how are classes?" before you even get it out of your mouth. DO NOT

ask these vague, general questions because you'll get only vague, general answers. DO NOT ask about class size. Instead, if that's important to you, ask the tour guide how many students were in his freshman English class. (Almost every school, somehow, manages to boast a 17-to-1 student-to-teacher ratio, or so they say, so the freshman English class will provide a more concrete gauge.) DO NOT ask what the social scene is like. Instead, ask what your tour guide did the previous evening. We've heard some stunningly candid responses to that one and answers infinitely more interesting than "we have a wide range of social clubs that represent over three dozen different . . . blah, blah, blah." Students have told us about documentaries they have filmed, late night snack businesses they have run, trans-gender balls they have attended, and make-out sessions with the boyfriend they have . . . well, you get the picture. The point is, ask specific questions, and you'll get specific—sometimes even colorful—answers.

## THE A TO Z GUIDE OF QUESTIONS TO ASK STUDENTS WHILE VISITING A CAMPUS
**(if you really want to get at the nitty gritty of a place . . .)**

A)  How many students were in your freshman English class?

B)  How many students are in one of the classes in your major now?

C)  What were you doing last night at, say, 10:00 pm? (Just to help get a sense of the campus climate . . .)

D)  What personal interactions have you had with any of your professors?

E)  What's your favorite professor like? Can you describe a memorable moment with him or her?

F)  Do you have any friends from out of state?

G)  How do you meet people?

H)  How does your advisory system work?

I)  Do you have any friends who've graduated and gotten jobs? What sorts of fields? What help does the college offer?

J) How are roommates chosen?

K) What is your living situation like? Are you guaranteed four years of on-campus housing?

L) What is one thing you'd change? If you could donate a million dollars to your college, where would you want it to go?

M) How do people who aren't members of fraternities or sororities socialize?

N) How safe is the campus? Do women feel safe walking alone at night? How about the surrounding areas? How are town-gown relations in general?

O) What are the popular extracurricular activities?

P) What is an interesting school tradition? How about haunted buildings?

Q) How are athletes viewed?

R) Do students talk about their classes a lot?

S) How many hours a day do you usually study?

T) How often do you use the library?

U) What service opportunities are there?

V) Have you studied abroad? Do you know anyone who has? Do study-abroad students typically live with host families or in dorms?

W) What sort of academic support is there?

X) How would you describe the diversity on campus?

Y) Is there an honor code? How does discipline happen?

Z) How much does teaching classes play into tenure? This last question would be if you happen to chat with a professor for a few minutes. It might not mean much to you, but it'll mean A LOT to him or her. In simple terms, the response will reveal how much real-world value an institution puts on educating its students.

(That's it. Just don't feel the need to ask these questions of one person, all at once!)

## THE INTERVIEW

Not every college interviews. Stanford, for example, never has, but for some, such as Denver University, the interview forms a hugely important part of the application portfolio. Check out the schools you're interested in either online or in the *Fiske Guide*, and see what each wants. If the interview is important, and there's no way you can visit before applying, call the school (and YOU should call, not your dad) to find out what else you can do. The school might suggest that you set up a meeting with the rep who'll come to visit your area, or maybe you could talk with a local alum. The different permutations of the interview are mentioned below. Whatever the interview, though, remember the one piece of advice a colleague gives to his advisees, "It's conversation, *not* interrogation."

### The Alumni Interview

The reality behind these is that, more than anything else, they're to make the alumni feel that they're still "in the loop" with their alma maters. Of course, if the interview goes either really well or bombs, the alum will let the school know. The fact that some of these alumni interviewers aren't exactly kept on a tight tether became clear to Eric when he saw one of his own advisees, post-interview.

"How'd it go?" he asked.

Looking visibly shaken, the student said, "Not very well."

Assuming she was about to start beating herself up for something she'd said that she was now second-guessing, Eric began the encouragement routine.

"No . . . it's not that," she said.

"Then what?"

"It's just that the guy . . . he lectured me about reincarnation for *three hours*. Is that normal?" she asked, voice trembling.

In another instance, the alum came to chat with one of Lynda's students at his home. The interviewer became so besotted with the student's attractive single mom that he stayed all afternoon, even wangling an invitation to dinner from that polite lady. Lynda dropped a short note to the admission office, explaining what had happened. It's no surprise that the college, once at the top of the student's list, dropped quite a few notches. So go to the alumni interview well dressed, and be your professional best, but don't start hyperventilating because, after all, the alum could be nuttier than you are.

### The Student Interview

Some colleges use students as their primary interviewers, but don't let this fool you. High school students, expecting some scary-looking older guy, relax when they see someone close to their age come out. Now, relaxing is good . . . relaxing too much is bad. The student interview should be taken just as seriously as if you were talking with the director of admission himself. Just the fact that the college student talking to you is cute and easy to chat with doesn't mean that it's ok for you to kick off your shoes and sit cross-legged on the couch.

### The Regular Admission Interview

First, remember that the admission rep is, more often than not, someone who's young and typically a recent graduate of the college you're visiting. Also, he or she wants you to like the school as much as you want to be liked. It's a sales pitch on both sides.

What do they want to see? This is when we say, "Be yourself . . . sort of." By "sort of," we mean be who you are, but a more polite version who speaks more clearly. Moms typically ask us what their child should wear for the interview. Lynda recalls an advisee, trying to make a good impression, who wore a three-piece wool suit to a July interview at Amherst, dripping with sweat. So, our standard response is "nice school clothes."

You want to know what sorts of things the admission reps write down when you enter? "Good poise . . . firm handshake." And, of course, they're probably doodling some, too. The admission rep wants to see that you're comfortable with yourself, and also—ready for the word again?—that you're "passionate." This is simply code for "interesting." Are you full of yourself? Are you a bland babbler? Or—heaven forbid—are you condescending? Try to get a sense of how you come across. If you're a pretentious lout, maybe this is a good time to figure that out. During the interview, you'll also want to ask a question or two—and not the sorts of questions that could be answered just by glancing at one of the college's brochures. Rather, think of something that really connects to your interests. Ask something specific about the music department if you like music. If you're into community service, ask what sorts of opportunities exist. For more ideas, look back at those A to Z questions.

## LAST TIPS

1) Never, EVER act in a condescending way during the interview—or, for that, matter, in life. No one likes it when someone else—but especially a teen—cops a 'tude.

2) Related to attitude, if your mother happens to open the door before the interview is over, DO NOT tear her a new one and gripe to the admission rep about how embarrassing she is. (This actually happens!) Remember that your behavior reflects who you are the whole time, not just during the Q & A. Interviewers have told us about seemingly sweet-natured applicants who turn into demon teens from hell when interacting with their parents. So note: if you're a kid who tells your mom to shut up, or even one who gets all huffy in public, reconsider how you're coming across. (Hint: Your mom isn't the embarrassing one in those instances, we promise . . .)

A parent from our school and mother of three kids who navigated this process exceptionally well offers her own special tips:

1) The night before the interview, review the information on the college's website so that you have the pertinent information in mind. Any interviewer will take you more seriously if you seem knowledgeable (and seriously interested) in the college.

2) Be sure to get the interviewer's card.

3) Buy a box of thank-you notes. Take it when you travel, and keep it in your desk at home. After the interview, *the very same day*, write a sincere note of thanks to your interviewer. It makes more of a difference than you'd ever imagine—you're no longer just the tenth appointment of the day, you're a stand-out!

Finally, the last but most important piece of advice for the interview: check your nose and your fly before going in.

## TYPICAL INTERVIEW QUESTIONS

1) What can you tell us about yourself that's not on your application?

2) Tell me about your school.

3) What are some of your academic strengths and weaknesses?

4) What is your favorite class this year?

5) What activity takes up most of your time this quarter (besides applying to college)?

6) What would you bring to our community?

7) What activities on our campus interest you?

8) What books do you have on your nightstand right now?

9) What did you do last weekend?

10) What questions do you have for us?

11) Why are you looking at me like that?

12) No, really . . . why?

### How to Prepare for the First Date

1) Don't overdo the cologne or perfume.

2) Don't even think about saying, "I love you."

3) Don't blow this out of proportion: it *is* just a date.

4) Know where you're going and how to get there.

5) Arrive on time—but not early.

6) Look your date in the eyes.

7) It's ok to touch, but mauling might not be the best idea.

8) Don't try to impress, or it'll come off as forced.

9) Be yourself . . .

10)  . . . unless you're not a very nice person, in which case you should be anyone else.

# Meet the Parents

How to let your parents have a say without their dominating your every waking thought

> *"A slavish bondage to parents cramps
> every faculty of the mind."*
> —MARY WOLLSTONECRAFT

This is the moment everyone's afraid of. You really like that special someone, but now it's time for that special someone's not-so-special parents to give you the once-over. In the college application world, you're not meeting anyone's parents, of course—except those of your new roommate—but your OWN parents are—and should be—a part of this process. On second thought, this whole deal can sometimes make your parents go so far off the deep end that it may *seem* as if you're meeting them for the first time. But back to the point. We say "part of" the process meaning just that: it is about YOU now, so don't let their expectations or unfulfilled dreams dictate how you handle your college choice. They had their chance, right? Now YOU'RE the one going to college.

Even your grandparents, the ones who have always defended you when your parents get crazy, slipped you extra spending money, and let you stay up all night if you wanted, can become strange. One seemingly-normal, very nice grand-dad cornered Lynda during a social lunch one day. He was concerned because his brilliant grandson, then a junior in high school, wasn't very interested in where he'd go to college. All this straight-A, perfect-tester, outstanding-in-every-way kid wanted to do was play music with his friends, and he figured he could do that at his local state college. This time, it wasn't mom who was worried, but grand-dad could only think about how much time the boy would be "losing" as he followed his not-so-academic interest. The older, experienced guy (a college prof himself, by the way), figured his grandson would wake up in ten years, sorry he hadn't gotten the right credentials from a fancy school by age 25.

You're at a time in your life when you're seeking independence, but you still need your parents' support, both emotional and financial. It's okay to admit this, and you should realize that basically, they just want the best for you. Parents do, however, have a tough time letting go. You're going to see aspects of these people you've known all your life that you never even suspected existed. Be patient, be understanding, and be ready!

Students: you might feel like your parents are the most embarrassing people on the planet, but usually they aren't as embarrassing as you think they are. The mother of one of our advisees, mid-tour, tripped, did an about-face, and fell onto a bush—which was made all the more awkward by the fact that her slacks fell down to her ankles, exposing flowery underpants and all. Now THAT'S awkward, but even still, these things happen.

The fact that your parents want to be a part of the process makes sense. After all, they'll likely be helping you a lot with the financial end of things. Beyond this, they love you. The problem comes when love turns into an obsessive need to control. The term the media has been tossing around lately to describe this more obsessive parent would be the "helicopter parent," because—you guessed it—they're always hovering. An article in *The Wall Street Journal* quoted Susan Lewis, a teacher at University of Maryland Eastern Shore, labeling the cell phone "the world's longest umbilical cord." And remember when we talked early on about that prestige disease? Turns out, because of their own brand of peer pressure, parents are more prone to catching this dreadful illness than their kids.

These overly-focused folks are the parents who are constantly at their children's side, never once allowing them to fall or fail in any way. Several college deans have explained to us that this hovering and nudging, while perhaps coming from a well-intentioned place, often has insidious consequences. Students who have been so over-programmed—going from the piano lesson to SAT class to the homeless shelter to church to club hockey practice—end up not developing much of an identity of their own, and when forced to do something by themselves, they honestly don't know which way to turn. When some of these teenagers leave the safety of their structured worlds and are allowed to fail in any way, they respond with pretty odd and frightening behavior. Colleges are seeing more stalking, binge-drinking, and even self-mutilation than ever before. Whether we're talking dating or college, none of that's good.

Of course, parents' backing off during the college admission process won't change a lifetime of over-involved behavior, but it's a start. If you think your parents might fit this description at all, leave this book out and open to this page to see if they pick it up. (They've likely already read it cover to cover.) Or you can just give it to them and ask them to read the following advice:

## A FEW WORDS FOR WELL-MEANING PARENTS

1) Don't ask other parents about their kids' GPA's, SAT scores, or list of colleges. It smacks of competition, and it's tacky. Also, don't talk about your own kid's scores, no matter how you feel about them. Avoid picturing the bumper sticker from an uber-selective college on the family Volvo. In "My Son the Number" in the April 20, 2008 *Education Life* section of the *New York Times*, Dulcie Leimback writes about her experience: "They [other parents] would try to tease out your child's score, as if digging for your age or income bracket. An otherwise modest father let it drop in a casual exchange in the grocery line that his son had done 'exceedingly well' on the SAT, studying my face for the jealous

flinch. Long pause. Now tell me yours." The author goes on to explain how her son, while never quite able to amaze anyone with his score, ended up just fine. The pressures, she suggests, are still very real.

2) If you feel yourself getting too pushy, or if your son or daughter is backing away and not telling you what's going on—with either the college process or life in general—know that this is normal. In many cases, the kid is working, getting the apps done, and just not wanting to tell you. In other cases, he's not. Either way, the second your son or daughter feels like you're about to nag—even if you aren't—you've lost contact. We've seen many instances in which the parents do start nagging, then the kid backs off, and the more the kid backs off, the more the parents nag . . . ad infinitum.

If this is starting to happen, you might determine one time a week—Sunday afternoons, say—that will be "college time." During any other moment, college talk will be off-limits. (Since really, Mom and Dad, though you mean well, your kid is getting it from every angle.) During "college time," however, you'll be able to find out what's really going on and how much (or little) your kid has done.

Offering another possibility, Dr. Beverly Morse, long-time admission director at Kenyon College (and a mom who has been through this process herself), suggests a 90-minutes-per-week limit on college talk. Her idea is that the time can be used in a block or parsed over several days.

3) As Jay Matthews, the education writer for the *Washington Post*, says in *Harvard Schmarvard*, parents are to "look but not touch." This is true for the essay or any other aspect of the application, and it's good advice. Hard as it is to stand back, the second you start getting your hands all over the application, it stops belonging to your son or daughter. We've even known of parents—at public high schools as well as private ones—who've gotten their secretaries to fill out the kid's application . . . which, as you'd imagine, would constitute another NO!

4) Be aware that odd stuff surfaces during this time. You're feeling the things you are for the right reason: simply, you want the best for your child. As Lynda has long been fond of saying, for you, your child's admission to college tends to feel like a report card on your parenting. Nevertheless, at this scary stage in your life, you'll need to muster all the self-discipline you have and trust your kid.

5) Did we mention the part about backing off *after* the apps are in the mail, too? The mother of one of Eric's students actually pretended to be her daughter when the college called so she'd get the acceptance information first. Remember that this is your child's process, and though he or she might not get everything right, the mistakes are for the kids to make.

6) Once your son or daughter is off to college, if you call each other once a day or more, you might consider giving a little more space. Remember the cell phone as umbilical cord metaphor? You don't have to know what color shirt Susie put on today nor should she feel the need to call and tell you.

7) Let your kid ask any questions, and in general, speak on his or her own behalf. While visiting USC, one proud but misdirected dad blurted out to the admission officer in front of a roomful of people, "My daughter's a real track star. You'll be glad you met her!" The girl looked like she wanted to disappear into the wall.

8) Tell yourself that too much pampering can lead, ultimately, to depression. Just as you wouldn't intercede on your kid's behalf after a broken heart and go after the ex, neither should you micromanage your child's academic life.

9) Don't forget that many kids' lives are so scheduled and programmed that they barely have time to know what they want. As a friend of Eric's, who teaches at an elite, super-selective university, noted, "My students are great, but they're also like perfect little machines."

10) Later on, if you'd even consider calling a professor to ask about a grade, we have just one piece of advice: DON'T! Let your kid handle the situation.

However, amid all this advice to step back and allow your child to become more independent, we need to offer a caveat: There ARE some instances when a parent needs to weigh in. During the admission process, there can exist pressures and promises from a college (Division I coaches come to mind) that kids really can't handle alone. Once the student is off to school, there are some cases where an adult voice is needed, as well. One of Lynda's advisees, a bright, capable, and very independent guy, as a new freshman was somehow mistakenly placed in a dorm full of grad students. Try as he might, he couldn't get anyone in authority to help him move, even for the second semester, to an undergrad dorm. The mom, having taken Lynda's philosophy about not smothering to heart, finally came to tell her about the problem. By now, the student had become so miserable that he was ready to drop out of college. Lynda's advice was simple: "Get on a plane; go to the dean's office, and don't leave until you have a promise that your child will get a new living situation, SOON!"

### What to Do When Meeting Your Date's Parents

1) Ask them questions about job, life, whatever, but don't talk all the time.

2) Shake hands and make eye contact.

3) However you were planning on dressing, notch it up one.

4) Yodel during dinner.

5) Or not.

Chapter 9

# The Love Letter

The application, essay, and other paperwork

*"I essay much, I hope little, I ask nothing."*
—Edward Elgar

Now you're almost ready to start what you've been avoiding all along: the writing. Though most of what we'll be talking about in this section is the personal-statement essay itself, there are a few other documents worth mentioning—such as the rest of the application.

## THE APPLICATION

Check to see which of the schools you're applying to take the Common Application (www.commonapp.org). This will save you a lot of time because you can use the same application to apply to many schools.

You can also save the app on your computer and send everything on-line, which most schools prefer.

There is some discussion about schools secretly wanting you to use their own application even if they take the Common App. We've looked into this with a number of places, and it's a fear that seems unfounded. Also, if you send the Common App, make sure that the school does, in fact, take it. Additionally—and this is important—check what supplemental writings each school wants. Even those that take the Common App will almost always want a little something else—such as a paragraph detailing why you want to attend Dorko State. The rest of the application is pretty much just filling out forms—pretty anticlimactic, according to most students. You fill out vital statistics, an activity roster (and yes, you may send a more complete sheet if you'd like, though it's generally not necessary), and then you've got the writing. Simple as that.

Three quick final thoughts. First, keep in mind that some reps have a saying: "A thick file represents a thick student." Simply, this means that it's not necessary to overwhelm the admission rep with paperwork detailing every aspect of your existence. Second, come clean with any discipline issues. If you've been suspended, it's infinitely better to state this yourself up front—along with how you've grown—than to try to hide it. Finally, make sure to use the same name on every part of the app. We've had students write "Alexandra" on one part and "Alex" on another, and guess what? Alex Alexandra ended up with two incomplete files in the admission office.

## THE SUPPLEMENTS

Even most of the Common App schools want a supplement of some sort or another, so check each college's website to see what it wants. Often, the question will have something to do with why you want to go to their school. Hint: DO NOT BLOW OFF THIS QUESTION.

Two aspects of these questions are important. First, many schools use these little paragraphs as secret litmus tests to see how a student really writes and thinks. Admission folks are on to the fact that most high school students go over their essays a jillion times, but they also know that most view these supplements as almost throw-away questions. As a result, the grammar might be more "honest" and the ideas less polished. Second, colleges use these questions to gauge the sincerity of a student's interest in attending. When responding to the supplements, as with the essay, be specific. *If a college wants to know what makes you invested in attending, don't just say that the campus is pretty and the classes are good. Drop two or three tangible, concrete reasons: a funky tradition the tour guide mentioned, a psychology professor you heard about, or even a popular cafeteria meal.* Anything specific is more meaningful than what some students tend to write here. It needs to be genuine because colleges realize that the Common App allows students to apply to a large number of schools with comparative ease. This supplemental response enables you to convince each college you apply to that you are genuinely interested. That's important because even the very hottest institutions are having a tougher time predicting who's going to attend out of their pool of admitted students.

## LOOSE ENDS

There's also usually a place to write a few lines about anything you'd like. It's for something you want to say that doesn't fit elsewhere on the application. Here's a chance to explain any little oddity that doesn't fit with the rest of your app—like the time you needed to go to the bathroom during the entire SAT Subject Test in physics and so you ended up with a 420, even though you'd earned an A+ in the class.

## ACTIVITIES LIST

This résumé of sorts isn't essential, but it can help if the application doesn't provide enough room for something legitimately worthy of additional explanation. Don't write up a whole activities list just because you didn't have space on the Common App to include that fourth-place award you got in eighth grade for the hot–dog-eating contest. Independent counselors (remember those guys from chapter four?) often over-emphasize this and have the student come up with an activities list that's just too slick. If you do it, make it your own.

## TEACHER RECOMMENDATIONS

If you attend an independent school, your counselor will likely be writing what's called the "school report," which is an overview of you as both a human being and a scholar (scary, right?). Beyond this, every applicant will generally need to ask two teachers for recommendations. Some students like to ask one humanities teacher and one math or science, but this usually isn't necessary (still, check each college's admission requirements to make sure). The most important thing about the rec letter is that the teachers know you well and have something positive to say. Obviously, if you bombed the class, that wouldn't be so good, but the letter doesn't necessarily have to be from a teacher who gave you an "A," either. Think of instructors you've had personal interactions with. These recommendation letters are not meant to be expansive overviews of you. Rather, they should provide a single teacher's perspective with maybe an anecdote or two. If you can't think of an individual teacher you've chatted with outside of class, then you need to change the way you relate to these important people. And don't think that talking to a teacher—who is, after all, sort of human-like—means you're brown-nosing. Believe it or not, most teachers got into teaching because they like teenagers (for some odd reason).

How about timing? A polite request would be good before the summer of senior year. Some teachers won't even think about writing until the fall, when you give them the forms they need, but others will actually start work that summer so they don't feel overwhelmed at the start of the following academic year. Note: if you ask a teacher for a recommendation, make sure you don't change your mind and not follow up. We've seen grumbly teachers say how they wrote a letter that was never used. ("I'd like to write *another* letter," they always say.)

Finally, regarding the recommendation letters: two is what most schools ask for, and two is enough. Some students like to flood the admission offices with recs from neighbors, friends, and first-grade coaches. Rather than being a help, this is only an irritant: college admission representatives have enough paperwork, and they don't need more. It isn't cute, and it doesn't make them smile. Now, if you have a super-special relationship with a former soccer coach who took you to Zambia where you performed brain surgery on a tribal chieftain, and that same coach asks you if she can write a letter, by all means include it. Similarly, if your grandmother is a trustee of the college, and she just donated the funds for a new building on campus, ask her to write that extra letter. Otherwise, keep things to a minimum. ***Please, please, please, don't forget a thank-you card and a small gift for the teachers who write your recommendations.*** The gift is important because first, it's a nice thing to do. Your teachers spend many hours during an already hectic time of year, taking precious time away from grading papers, being with family, and watching *American Idol*, to think about YOU. Second, if you drop off the note and thank-you gift a week or two before the rec's due date, they will actually serve as a polite reminder to the teacher to write that letter and get it in the mail. (Like that? Kill two birds with one stone!)

By the way, when you give your teachers the rec request, don't just chuck it on his or her desk. Rather:

1) Print out the teacher recommendation form and fill out ALL the information you can—including the teachers' address (which would be the school's address, since teachers don't really have a life outside of school anyway . . .).

2) Check the box that says you waive the right to see the reference letter, which is important. If a college thinks there's even a chance the student was hovering over the teacher's shoulder during the writing of the rec letter (either literally or figuratively), the letter is meaningless.

3) Include a stamped envelope for each form (self-stick is a nice touch) addressed to the admission office of the corresponding college.

4) Put all in a neat little packet with the due dates for *each* application clearly marked.

## THE TRANSCRIPT

Your school registrar will be sending this out, but be sure to ask to check it over in advance, looking for mistakes or problems. Get any errors corrected, and explain anything that needs explaining in the space just for that purpose on the app. Fill out a transcript request form with each college's address and the due dates for the school's registrar. You'll likely need to address medium-sized envelopes and slap two stamps on each.

## ONLINE STUFF

It's important to be careful here. We include this category because, just as many employers are now checking the blogs and MySpace accounts of potential employees, so, too, are some colleges. Keep in mind that what you write online exists for all the world to see, so the rule is this: if you wouldn't say it out loud at a family reunion, don't put it on the web. Also, if you've got a knucklehead email handle like "bonghitdude," change it. (Seriously, bonghitdude.)

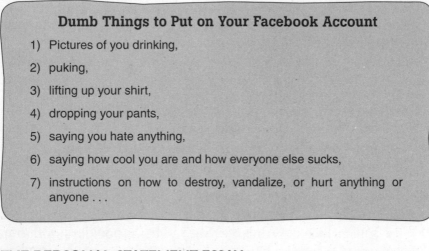

**Dumb Things to Put on Your Facebook Account**

1) Pictures of you drinking,

2) puking,

3) lifting up your shirt,

4) dropping your pants,

5) saying you hate anything,

6) saying how cool you are and how everyone else sucks,

7) instructions on how to destroy, vandalize, or hurt anything or anyone . . .

## THE PERSONAL STATEMENT ESSAY

Yes, this is it. What you've been waiting for. Tips on how to write the essay . . . (You can hardly express your excitement, right?)

1) In general, don't send poetry as your essay. It rarely works. And yes, one of Lynda's former students did do this and brilliantly, but it just so happens the girl was the best writer Lynda ever taught in her 37-year career.

2) Yes, yes, you know now to "be yourself," but with the essay, how that translates is this: think of a cool something you did and write about it as if you were telling it to a friend. Eliminate the "ums" and "likes" later, but what you have on that piece of paper is your voice. Restructure it and you might have something.

3) If the essay sounds like it could be read by the movie voice-over guy, it's not your voice.

4) Remember that most college admission people read your essay while they're lying on the couch, at home, with a baby crying in the background and dinner burning; and besides, they've already read forty essays that afternoon. They want to read something fun and interesting and refreshing, but they're not seeing it. Not yet. If you picture that admission rep in this context, it'll help you find that original voice. Figure out how to make that rep glad she's reading what *you* wrote!

5) One high school teacher suggested this for essay topics: write down the first three ideas that come into your head. Then cross those out. Chances are, everyone else thought of those ideas, too. We'd suggest carrying around a note card. Then, whenever you have a flash, jot it down. Wait a week or so, look at your scribbles, and decide if you have a workable topic.

6) The essay needs to be a "slice of life." Avoid moralizing, because believe us: the admission person isn't reading your essay for advice.

7) Keep in mind that most admission people read your essay in one to two minutes. This, of course, seems discouraging after all the work you put into it, but think of it this way: just as a TV commercial has only a few seconds before you decide if you're going to change the channel, so, too, does your essay have to grab your reader fast.

8) The essay usually won't stop a good candidate from getting in, nor will it make a school roll out the red carpet for someone who's otherwise weak. It will make whoever's reading it take a second look at your app. A colleague at another school was working with a student who, fantastic as she was in class, kept turning in bland essay drafts. The writing piece, which was on "someone I admire," was about her cousin. The original draft of the essay recounted how much she liked and respected him. And on and on. After one read, our colleague looked the student over and asked a point-blank question: "When you were little, did you have a crush on your cousin?" The student realized that yes, she had, and changed the essay's opening line to the following: "I fell in love for the first time when I was five. Unfortunately, it was with my cousin." Admission folks apparently were passing that one around for days. Of course, this is not to say that you need to be weird. That particular student simply tapped an honest vein, and as good writing is supposed to do, it became a self-revelatory experience—and one that was also fun.

9) Avoid receiving hands-on help with your writing. By all means, a teacher or counselor can read it to provide "big picture" suggestions, but even this should be a discussion rather than a "how to"

session. Many schools are on to the fact that a number of applicants are getting more help on their essays than they should. As a result, a few colleges have even begun comparing the SAT essay with the formal one. If the latter seems too "scrubbed," it'll raise suspicion. (And rightfully so, might we add.)

10) You've probably already heard that there are several cliché formulas that students use when writing, such as the study abroad formula where the student ends by saying how much she learned about another culture. Or the sports-as-metaphor-for-life essay, which throws around a lot of words like "goals," "obstacles," "overcome," and "victory." The only word we'd use for these sorts of essays, however, is: "B-O-R-I-N-G." Your reader will watch *Rudy* again if he's in the mood for triumphant sports stories. Simply, you should not write an Important-with-a-capital-"I" essay.

While such "Important" essays have no place in a college admission application, this doesn't mean you can't talk about a meaningful study abroad experience or something that happened to you on a playing field. You can tell these stories—indeed, that study abroad trip might truly have been a turning point for you—but if you do, think back to what you talked about with your friends after you returned. THAT'S the story you want to tell. Honestly, can you imagine coming back from Argentina and telling your best friend: "This was an eye-opening trip for me because I learned that, despite our cultural differences, we . . ." NO!

On the opposite end of the spectrum, one of Lynda's advisees, Helen, wrote about one of those BIG life-changing experiences. She'd just come back from a summer of community-service and language study where she lived with a family in a tiny Dominican village near the Haitian border. How did she approach it so that the reader didn't yawn? Helen wrote a hilarious piece about learning to cheat at cards from her new brothers and sisters. Not only did it match up nicely with her "12" on the essay portion of the SAT writing test, but the rep from the college where Helen had applied ED remembered the piece so vividly that she later mentioned it in a phone call to Lynda. The second you tell a real story about your life, it's no longer cliché or formula. It's all you, and that's what counts.

11) Avoid some of those vague-sounding BIG words. A former student, Odysseus, wrote an essay on skydiving. He started off great. It was personal, with details about the color of the suit, his trembling hands, the smell of gasoline coming from the plane. But then he headed off into cliché-land, attempting to teach some big lesson. He started using phrases like "combat your fears," "follow your dreams," and "anything is possible." Eric had him go back and just tell the story.

12) Remember to be a human, not a hero.

13) Be honest, but as with the interview, don't feel like you need to bare every aspect of your soul. Perhaps you've overcome depression, but this is a tough topic to discuss because anything that suggests "emotional instability" scares admission people off. We've seen that happen more than once.

14) Humor is good, but be aware that all sorts of people may be reading your essay. If you think a word or phrase might offend, leave it out. One of Lynda's students wanted to write about a bungee-jumping adventure. Fine. But when he opted to include something about the way the safety harness felt on the more personal parts of his anatomy, Lynda reminded him that all his readers wouldn't likely be fourteen-year-old boys.

15) Don't pose, strut, or preen.

16) Use clear grammar and words you'd normally use when speaking.

17) Your opening gives that first impression that you won't get a second chance to make.

18) Your closing is the last opportunity to stick in the reader's mind.

19) Read essays by Joan Didion, E.B. White, George Orwell, and any other great essayist your English teacher might recommend.

20) Ground your writing more in verbs than adjectives—the usual favorite choice of high school writers. Also, don't forget about

the power of nouns—the more specific, the better. (The "tibia" is better than "a bone," "tuberculosis" is better than "a disease," and "Rottweiler" is more image-inducing than "doggie.")

21) Leave sentimentality behind. Trying to pull on the rep's heart strings by talking about the death of your pet goldfish will come off as forced and dull.

22) Don't argue like you're on the Speech and Debate team. The personal essay is not the time or place to set up a legal case. Only talk about "Important" topics if there's a real and personal connection to you.

23) Think about structure. You might have a great essay somewhere in your rough draft, but all you need to do is switch a few paragraphs around. Often, students will have a real zinger of an action paragraph buried in the heart of the essay—which the reader won't get to because she'll already be asleep by then.

24) Think about the importance of scene. In good writing, explanations are never as interesting as the details and action of the moment.

Note that we're mainly talking about the Common Application here. Some colleges will make you write much, much more in some arcane ways. Although this practice may seem sadistic, it's often their way of trying to probe more deeply into what makes you tick, how well you can write with severe word limitations, and, yes, just how badly you want to apply.

*Keep a copy of everything you send to the colleges, whether electronically or on paper, both on your computer and on a print-out.* Admission offices are busy places, and it's not uncommon for some part of your app to go astray. Be prepared to re-send anything you've done.

## A FEW SAMPLE ESSAYS TO SHOW YOU WHAT WE MEAN
Okay, you've heard all the rules and tips about how to write, but how does it actually translate to reality? We've asked a few of our brave students to share their essays, so here we go . . .

### The No-Idea-Where-to-Start Essay

A kind-hearted student, John, entered Eric's office one day, clearly flummoxed.

"I don't have any idea what I should write about," John said.

"What's something you've done you like to talk about?" Eric asked him.

"Well . . ." he, said, a little unsure of himself. "I've worked at Jamba Juice for a long time. But that wouldn't be good for an essay, would it?"

"Any stories?" Eric pressed.

And John talked. At first, the stories seemed to be disconnected anecdotes. He shared how embarrassed he had been by the fact that his car was nicer than those of the regular workers at Jamba Juice. Then there was the security guard who ordered the same drink every morning after getting off his late-night shift. And the weird goop that had to be cleaned from behind the fridge. More than just random stories, each was a vignette that said something about John's attitude about life. Though it didn't win him a Pulitzer, it did do something almost as important: it communicated his voice.

---

The air is cold and dry. It rushes down my lungs with every breath I take. My fingers are frozen, and they struggle to hold the metal tongs. Just one more apple cinnamon pretzel, and I can leave the confines of Jamba Juice's freezer. Along with learning to not spend too much time in the freezer, I had many lessons during my first summer job at a popular fruit smoothie shop in Denver.

The first lesson I learned at Jamba Juice was to never unplug a refrigerator with wet hands. Unfortunately, since it took me a while to fully understand this little detail, I spent part of my shift being almost electrocuted on the floor as my fellow "team members" nervously watched and waited for the manager before any of them would try to yank the plug from the wall. I also learned that there are jobs worse than cleaning a bathroom, such as cleaning corroded copper pipes underneath the counter. My third lesson was to always make sure there was plenty of our protein boost in stock, which proved especially true when the body builder/security guards from a neighboring hospital would come for their regular dosage of açaí and protein. I will never forget their—I hoped good-humored—tirade when we did not have any protein. Another lesson I learned was that a corporate think tank can be just as corny as a geometry textbook that has a chapter on "Rex Tangle," a lonely rectangle that just wanted to fit in . . . to a circle. The company's mantra, for example, was Fun, Integrity, Balance, Empowerment, and Respect, which stood for the awe-inspiring FIBER acronym. The district manager tested my knowledge of this acronym on a regular basis.

But these are only some of the learning experiences from my first job. Other lessons during that summer were more complex. While my electric shock experience was a practical lesson, I did learn a lot about myself and the world beyond my comfort zone, as well.

One girl I worked with was 17 and lived in a group home with her baby. I remember telling my dad one night that I felt guilty working there because I only needed money to pay for car insurance. I was one of the few to drive to work. My car, a dark blue 1999 Subaru Outback, was not flashy, but I still felt guilty driving it. Every day I parked it in the back of the parking lot, where no one would see it. Even though I was often worried about how my team members saw me, we still formed strong friendships. To them I was the sweet and innocent one in my first job. My manager trusted me enough to launch scoops of sorbet and frozen yogurt over his shoulder and have me catch them in a blender.

I also became aware that distant yet relevant problems are ignored every day. For example, we ran out of mango juice because of a drought in South America. The livelihoods of South American farmers were destroyed, while at our store customers were momentarily annoyed that their smoothies would be without mango juice. I never expected to learn a lesson about global economies at my little Jamba Juice store on 6th and Broadway, but since there was no news coverage, I would have overlooked the drought myself.

Finally, I learned that the secret to a good smoothie is just that—a secret. I memorized every single recipe for all the smoothies from strawberry tsunamis to peach pleasures. I would like to tell you them, but I'm sworn to secrecy.

---

What do we learn about John from this essay? He comes off as a sweet-natured guy with a self-deprecating sense of humor, and that's exactly who he is. Also, his subtle sarcasm pops up at a few points, especially in the opener, where he plays with the reader's expectations that he's on a mountain peak, about to overcome some great obstacle.

Eric talked to the admission officer of John's first-choice school after John had been accepted, and the officer said he had liked the sincerity in John's voice. There was no pretense or need to impress in that essay. It was all him.

## A Before-and-After Essay

This second essay was written by a wonderful student (though he'd be embarrassed by our calling him that) named Alex. Along with being a young academic, Alex is also a perfectionist, so we knew the essay was not something he was particularly looking forward to. This would be no last minute, fly-by-the-seat-of-the-pants experience for him, no siree. He shared the essay below for Eric's feedback.

### Alex Essay #1

Picture a gleaming Tootsie Roll Pop. Fixed to a chalky paper stick sits a perfectly proportioned globe of rigid, sparkling sugar with a chewy center. The key is to dissolve the lollipop completely, taking time to enjoy the hard candy shell, the sticky center, and the sweet layers in between. Similarly, life is relished when the aesthetic and artistic are grasped along with the objective and scientific beneath. Passionate about violin performance, foreign language, and medicine, I live my life as I would eat a Tootsie Roll Lollipop.

The sweet sounds of violin and classical music are my lollipop's outer layers. I began my journey in violin performance at age four, when the only musical piece I could "play" was an overly simplified version of "Twinkle-Twinkle Little Star." I recall my four other family members' wincing with soured looks each time I picked up my instrument. Perhaps they believed at the time that my lollipop was lemon. I always just assumed their lollipops were bitter. However, fourteen years later, I performed Tchaikovsky's "Symphony #4" on an international orchestra tour in the heart of Buenos Aires with one of the most highly esteemed youth orchestras in the country. It enthralls me to be able to produce something so effective from a network of black dots printed on a page. Composers rarely depict a distinct image of what their music is meant to portray. Like a lollipop, a piece of music takes on many different flavors and consistencies. In art, there are never factual answers, only facades. In reality, though, there is more in life than just what is observed. The Tootsie Roll in the center of the pop is much more flavorful and enticing, but reaching it takes more than a simple satisfaction with a taste of its casing.

Serving as a Spanish-to-English interpreter for the physicians of a local hospital in Denver moves me beyond the lollipop's frame toward the Tootsie Roll, the true sustenance of the pop. Through foreign language, I use my artistic side as a means to better understand my scientific side. I spend many hours in the hospital, breaking the barrier between the Spanish-speaking patients and their physicians. Linguistic skills slice through the lollipop's shell to expose its core. Not only do they break the shell between patient and doctor, but they allow me to observe the procedures and techniques that the doctors perform so diligently. Since childhood, as the son of a physician, medicine has been my dream. I gain great excitement from problems that cannot be fixed comfortably. The first answer in medicine is not necessarily correct, just as the first lollipop pulled off the shelf may not be as tempting as another. Every perception and thought process is required to perform a doctor's job well. Each challenge that a doctor comes upon is just another layer of a lollipop to be broken down. However, this inherent thought process practiced regularly in medicine is the means by which the layers to be dissolved. As each roadblock is overcome in medicine, ten different questions are answered. Inevitably, science is the systematic, objective tool that will dislodge the Tootsie Roll.

High SAT scores do not conquer the lollipop of life. Perfecting Sibelius's "Violin Concerto" doesn't either. It is essential to apply both areas of expertise. Without diversity, the lollipop either stays in its wrapper or breaks into indiscernible pieces. I think I've learned how to take my time with the lollipop of life, and I'd love to use these skills effectively in college over the next four years.

---

But what's wrong with that?, you might be asking yourself. Clearly, the guy's a solid writer, he's a good student, and he's got some great life experiences, too. (This all says nothing of the fact that he has more musical talent in his pinky finger than in most people's whole body!) So let's break it down. First, what sort of voice do you hear when reading the essay? Is it a voice you'd want to have a coffee with? Maybe, maybe not. Alex is actually a funny, self-effacing guy—someone you actually probably *would* want to have a coffee with—but this first essay captures none of who he really is. Rather, it offers a slightly rehashed version of his activities roster, in the guise of a rather convoluted lollipop metaphor. Sure, Alex is technically a decent writer here. There are no real grammar problems nor spelling mistakes, but the image of the lollipop might confuse the reader. Does Alex have a hard candy shell with a sticky center? And does he have a stick up his . . . you get the idea. Also, real-world Alex has an impressive vocabulary; even still, words like "artistic," "aesthetic," "scientific" and "objective," when strung together don't sound like him—especially when combined with the passive voice. (Remember that from your English teachers?)

Suddenly, this smart, interesting guy appears distant and formal; his real voice barely squeaks through.

"Tell me," Eric said, "about that Argentina trip last summer."

"But wouldn't that be cliché?" Alex asked.

"Not if it's really a story you'd tell."

Eric remembered how many stories Alex had wanted to tell after the Argentina trip, stories that were a little offbeat, and stories that were also all him. They were funny in that "can you believe this happened to me?" sort of way. Eric pushed a little.

"Can you think of any of those stories you were most excited about telling? What were some of *those*?"

Eric and Alex chatted. Alex unfurled a litany of sad-sack stories that made Eric genuinely laugh.

"But won't those be too negative?" Alex asked.

"You have a good point. You don't want to come off as a whiny tourist, because you're not. Simply tell the story just as you told it to me."

Alex did. A week later, he returned with this version:

### Alex Essay #2

"¡Son mis violines! ¡Son mis violines!" yelled the Argentine would-be robber on our tour bus. With three violins in each hand, the young man fell forward as the conductor of our orchestra clobbered him. The next moment, he who had been so desperate to take advantage of 100 American musicians, now sat whimpering on the floor of the bus stopped between the Hotel Broadway and the towering obelisk of Buenos Aires.

On each day of its tour in Argentina, my orchestra embarked at 11:00 AM to rehearse in yet another concert hall, set to please engaged audiences each night. Evidently, the local pickpockets caught on to the schedule quickly. I am a person normally adamant about maintaining my composure; the robo de violines was thankfully the last event of many that tested my sanity during those amazing 21 days in Argentina.

I like to live by a structured schedule, and I knew right from the start that I wouldn't be able to do so on this trip. Only days before we encountered the robber on our bus, the pilot's voice rang from the speakers in the 747 bound to Buenos Aires, saying that there was heavy fog in the Buenos Aires area that would prevent our scheduled landing. Along with 160 other inbound flights, ours landed at the single-runway airport in Córdoba—on the other side of the country. The crew assured us that all we had to do was refuel for a later flight. We would leave in no more than thirty minutes. However, after thirty minutes, the weather was no better and we went nowhere. The pilots could no longer fly legally because their maximum hours of flight time were up. Also, we could not leave the plane because the minuscule terminal was at maximum capacity. And, of course, only two Argentine bag handlers were working that day.

Nine hours later, we loaded our instruments onto a bus for the eight-hour drive across the 710 kilometers of Argentine desert. As four of us sat down in the front row of the second level and rested our feet on the metal foot bar attached directly to the front window, the glass shattered into pieces. We didn't make it to Buenos Aires that day; in fact, we wouldn't reach the city for a week.

After 27 hours of exhausting travel, a trip across the freezing, wintry Argentine pampa at two in the morning woke me up . . . literally. I am the sort of person who operates more efficiently when I know explicitly what is expected of me and what I expect of myself. If I am on time to an event, as far as I am concerned, I am already late. So having absolutely no choice but to accept the situation passively was difficult for me, to say the least. Just as we departed from Córdoba, I immediately fell asleep—barely. Do you know what it feels like to have your sleep interrupted so suddenly that nausea sets in? The red speed control siren in the new bus taught me this feeling immediately. Every time the bus driver exceeded 90 km/hour, a giant red strobe light went off, accompanied by the shrill, whining scream of a siren. Because we had to make 710 kilometers in a reasonable amount of time, the siren never ceased. Our faces soured and our stomachs twirled as each sound wave hit us. I used my Spanish to speak with the bus driver to see if there was anything he could do about the light. No luck. "Es la ley de Argentina," he said; it was the law. All I remember is that I thought to myself that there was no love of mine, even music, that would ever make up for this.

Two weeks later, however, I looked up at the bright lights of the symphony hall in the heart of Buenos Aires. The audience gave its eighth standing ovation of the night. After performing several successful concerts throughout the country, I just smiled. Had I been asked two weeks earlier about my expectations for the concerts, I probably would have rolled my eyes in sheer annoyance. I smiled that last night because everything was in order. I smiled not because I had learned some huge life lesson about patience or diversity. I smiled because I was astonished that I, the one person who was always worried about the future, was living in the now. I left past mishaps in the past. I smiled because the little girl in the front row and the elderly lady in the back smiled, hands clapping. Their smiles made me smile, and I realized that even I could move beyond my rigid life and enjoy that moment. With the echo of the audience's applause and that feeling still in my head, I only laughed when I walked into the deserted Buenos Aires airport and an employee looked at me and said bluntly, "No flights are leaving here tonight. Another storm is rising!"

---

Eric read it and smiled. The essay even *sounded* like Alex. It had his trademark humor, his wry pessimism. So he took an essay which didn't really offer much of that "slice of life" stuff we've been talking about and turned it into a real glimpse of his world.

## A Slice-of-Life Essay

Another wonderful student—there's that word again, but it's true—is Annabeth. While we don't have a "before" and "after" for her (indeed, her work happens in private, mysterious places), one of her primary essays was what you see below. We've included it because, while those life-changing moments are great to talk about, there are also millions of other life moments that are essay-worthy. Joseph Epstein, award-winning professional essayist, has a whole piece about napping, another about reading, and another about name-dropping. Boring? Hardly. He simply takes pieces of life and talks about them in a way everyone can relate to. In one of the essays in his book *Narcissus Has Left the Pool*, he describes his writer's voice as being very similar to the voice he'd use to write friends letters. That's the voice you want. And that, as you'll see below, is a voice Annabeth has found here:

### "The Best Things in Life Are Free"

I live in a grocery store – at least, according to most of the staff at Whole Foods.

To be fair, my visits usually average only a few times a week, and I find that I still spend most of my nights in my own bed. No, I'm not a devoted employee, and, no, I'm not stalking the cute barista. Whole Foods has become an after-school routine for me, a therapeutic, tranquil, tasty stroll through one very large, well-supplied pantry. It certainly helps that whoever designed this organic paradise decided on an exceptionally convenient location: only a few hundred feet from my backyard.

After months of smiling at the same faces, I came to the worrisome conclusion that every employee in the store recognized me . . . and my undeniable love for free food. I used to fret; their knowing nods and grins were somewhat disconcerting. True, I often came without money or the slightest intention of making a purchase, and to be fair, I may have taken more than a modest amount of sample chocolate. But, gradually, the staff seemed to accept me as a part of the store itself. The grins turned to waves and heartfelt greetings. Maybe all it really takes to develop a relationship with someone is time, because the half hour I spend after school – reading outside on the benches or choosing a new flavor of tea to try – was all it took to connect me to these people. The only common ground necessary was love for a store dedicated to environmental action and free Izze tastings.

One rather loud man who works in the fish department was the first to approach me about my regular presence. I've long since stopped being startled by his booming, always disbelieving shout of "You're here again?" but at first, I worried that this greeting was meant in an unfriendly manner. Consequently, I took to dodging behind the soup stand whenever I spotted his trademark goatee and yellow pants. My worry vanished after a school-sponsored stay in Argentina. I returned one month later to an exceptionally warm welcome and a relieved, "Where were you? We thought you'd left us!"

My favorite employees, though, may be my friends in produce and not just because they're the first ones you see upon entering the store. These few, worthy individuals face the exhausting job of stacking peaches into pyramids and identifying pluots and golden raspberries for the fruit-and-vegetable illiterate, not to mention their faultless refilling of the fruit salad samples. Every one of them is shockingly distinctive, both in appearance and personality. For example, one man could easily be a football quarterback: it's a wonder his broad shoulders fit through the relatively narrow space between aisles. Another produce expert possesses a head so full of dreadlocks that he's impossible not to spot among the cornucopia of ripe pineapples and juicy clementines. And finally, there's Brad, another long-time employee whose eyes squint up in a smile whenever I see him. They all seem to find my constant visitations humorous – a sentiment I'm only perpetuating with my ever-cheerful waves.

In the bakery, you'll find Rick, a man who once tried to set a Guinness World Record for how high he could toss pizza dough. (I was a witness to this one-time event. The dough in question almost adhered to a low-flying fluorescent light. It was quickly put away before anyone else could spot the twirling weapon.) Behind the dessert counter is Patricia, an expert at cutting a chocolate decadence cake into perfect portions for sampling, and at the coffee bar is Beth, a tired teenager who used to confess to me in quiet tones, "I'm hung over. Just don't tell my manager."

I've also struck up conversations with fellow shoppers and samplers. There's something to be said for the communal bonding power of standing around a chip bowl, quietly munching on handmade wheat chips and sampling each of the four types of homemade salsa and guacamole. Once, I was dipping into the brightly painted dish for some corn chips, but to my chagrin, the vessel was empty. I was ready to walk away, chalking this up as just another of the many lessons learnt at Whole Foods – live with disappointment, there's usually a cheese sample around the corner – but, to my surprise, an elderly man glimpsed the frustration etched in my frowning features. In another moment, he'd hurried over to rip open a full bag of chips to tip into the sample dish. "That's what they're there for," he grunted, smiling as he snagged one for himself and turned back to his cart.

Not only has Whole Foods exposed me to a fascinating selection of people, but after two years of devoted tasting, I think I've learned something about food. I'm certainly a connoisseur of French cheeses and internationally grown pesticide-free produce, and I've faithfully tried everything from chipotle caramels to goji berry juice. I've become a veritable tour guide of the bulk foods aisle, and I've learned that free radicals actually are bad for your health. I know that there are more than ten different types of organic frozen waffles. I've discovered that people really will spend seventy dollars on a bottle of weight loss formula, and I've determined the proper way to open a pomegranate. Learning about food, life, and people – what more could I ask for from an organic marketplace?

Ultimately, I know that walking the "geezer route," as my pre-calculus teacher lovingly termed the sample stroll, might sound trivial to one unfamiliar with the inner workings of a supermarket. But I don't really care: tonight there were three types of free chocolate.

---

So Annabeth has taken something as un-earth-shattering as her trips to Whole Foods and offered us a real glimpse of who she is. Is that a voice you'd like to get to know? Very likely. There's nothing didactic or moralistic about it. Rather, she simply shares a piece of her life. And what do we learn about her? Beyond the fact that she's a good writer, grounding her ideas in real specifics, we also learn that she's observant, that she has a wry, ironic sort of humor, and that she doesn't take herself too seriously. After all, anyone who could talk about "free Izze tastings" and finding connections with strangers in the same paragraph *has* to have a good sense of balance. The second you think she's going to veer into moral-land, she balances the statement with an image or a light touch of humor. Even still, Annabeth is not writing about something entirely trivial to her. The Whole Foods visits actually do represent a big part of her life! One college admission officer even emailed Annabeth a nice note, letting her know how much he had enjoyed the essay—not a bad sign!

## An Essay That Deals with Tragedy

The previous essays have dealt with smaller moments in life, but this is not to say that your essay must deal with the minutia of the day-to-day. Every year, students approach us with essays that deal with something deeply personal—tragic, even—and we talk with them about how to begin writing. We suggest that students avoid the tragic moments if the emotion is still too raw or if they haven't gotten over the event yet. Colleges don't need to see that you're Pollyanna Positive about whatever happened, but they do want to see that you've grown. They want to see the effect the event had on you, and they want to see how you handled it.

A former student of both Eric and Lynda's, a charismatic young woman at our school, Samantha, wrote an essay that deals with an event more stunningly tragic than most could imagine: her mother's suicide. In the essay, as you'll see, Sam didn't gloss over the intensity of her emotions, but she didn't dwell on the bleakness of the topic, either. Sam is a gentle, kindhearted student, and both of these qualities come out in her essay—not an easy feat when talking about feelings of such overwhelming magnitude.

----

She left us. She left me. I never thought I could be mad at someone for dying, but when my mom killed herself, I felt abandoned and angry. In her suicide note, she wrote she had "a black brain." This "black brain" stole my dearest companion from me when I was eleven.

Right about the time I was taking my first steps, my mom plopped me on the back of a horse. When I was old enough to steer my own pony, my mom and I rode side by side on the trail. Hiding away in our secret place, we would dismount our horses and have picnics in the lush summer grass. At the time, I did not like her horse, Little Boy, because he was wild and shabby looking. He threw his head high in the air as he galloped and always had bite marks from fighting with other horses.

When my mom died, I suddenly had to ride both my horse, Diamond, and her horse, rebellious Little Boy. One of our first expeditions resulted in Little Boy's galloping along Belleview Avenue, while I lay face down in the middle of a field. Eventually, Little Boy was apprehended by a police officer. Little Boy has settled down since his criminal days, and now he is my day-to-day companion and closest friend. He has become my memory of my mother. In some ways, Little Boy's affection towards me emulates the adoration my mom gave me. Only when I walk into the pasture does he stop kicking the other horses and trot over to greet me. I feel connected to my mom through the soothing sound of crunching carrots and the smell of Little Boy's breath after a peppermint treat. My mom's death was the catalyst that caused my passion for horses to grow.

As a result of my mom's death, I also evolved emotionally. I became more empathetic, better able to understand and comfort others. Because I have experienced tragedy firsthand, I am better able to appreciate my friends' deepest feelings. Beyond the emotional repercussions of my mom's absence, there are also practical ramifications. I am responsible for my own life. I schedule doctors' appointments for myself and veterinary appointments for Little Boy. When Little Boy and I competed in the Junior Olympics, I even had to get him a passport. While I do have a serious side, in school I am often described as the "comic relief" because I enjoy cheering people up. On the first day of school this year, I induced much laughter when I brought my costumed Little Boy to take part in the senior parade. Although I would have never asked for my mom to die, she did leave me, and I decided to grow rather than suffer from my losses.

My mom changed my soul in ways that not even I can understand. However, I do know that I would not be the person I am today had she not fostered a passion for horseback riding in me. Some of my greatest triumphs and happiest moments have been atop a horse. My mom wished for me to experience the incomparable sensation I feel when Little Boy and I are floating in the air over a jump. During the split second in which we are suspended in the air, I feel clarity, and I know this unparalleled feeling is my mom's gift to me. Little Boy is my connection to my mother, and the barn is a place where I find peace within myself. My mom's gift of riding helps me face the challenges that each day may hold. I can overcome the obstacles thrown my way in the same way I climb back into the saddle after Little Boy bucks me off, knowing they will only make me stronger.

---

Certainly, this essay is powerful, but in the wrong hands, it could have muddled the writer's voice, becoming too dark or moral-driven. Indeed, at the end, though she does say that she's stronger now, it doesn't come off as cliché or trite by any stretch of the imagination. She's a young woman we absolutely believe.

## A Life-Changing-Moment Essay

Of course, life-changing moments come in many forms. One student at our school, Haley, is a vegetarian, and in her essay she wrote about what led her to be the person she is now. As you'll notice, she grounds her writing in details and specifics—a theme you've likely noted in all the good essays—and she doesn't veer into the realm of the didactic. From the opening page, due to the simplicity of the story and its emotional force, the reader is hooked.

---

The burning iron rod sizzled on the skin of each wailing calf, and the smell of burning cowhide lingered in the air during branding season in LaGrange, Wyoming. It was the ranching event of the year. Every rancher in Bear Creek had come to help brand the new calves. With my jeans tucked into my cowboy boots, old shirt hanging out of my jeans, and my bent cowboy hat, I walked down to the old wooden fence surrounding the arena. Yes, I knew before I arrived that it was branding weekend, but what did that mean? Why were the calves in separate corrals from their mothers, bawling for help?

On that day in 1998, I first came to the realization that branding was the process of marking animals on their hides with a hot rod to show ownership. It deeply disturbed me to see those four-month-old calves, separated from their mothers, screaming in pain. As I walked away from the horrific smell, I wondered if there was another way to mark an animal besides branding.

Shortly after I discovered the brutality of branding, another incident took place that deeply disturbed me. We had a young calf, Charlie, who had been rejected by his mother. Charlie was uncommon: his chalky white body was accented by a pink nose, and he was gentle and affectionate with all the people he loved. I bottle-fed him twice a day. Each time I would clang the rusty tin cowbell, Charlie would come running with his short tail swinging behind him. I adored Charlie, and feeding him was the highlight of my day. Toward the end of the summer, he disappeared. The foreman, I discovered, had shipped Charlie to the feed lot. Charlie the calf became meat, and I became a vegetarian and a steadfast advocate for animal rights.

Since that day, I have not eaten any meat, poultry, or fish. For me, it was about more than food. Instead, it was always about animal rights. I knew I could make a difference by not only being a thoughtful consumer but by trying to convince my dad and other ranchers to put an end to recreational hunting on their lands. During dinners and barbeques, while the ranchers were working in the corrals and even during hayrides, I pushed and campaigned for all of the ranchers to end recreational hunting. It took some work and persistence. Finally, I was exhilarated when my dad agreed, and then many of the other ranchers joined with him. Hunting in our area has almost completely stopped, with the exception of hunting overpopulated wild turkey. I feel a deep sense of accomplishment knowing that I have saved many lives that most likely would have been taken.

In addition, I have joined the United States Animal Protection Group, a nonprofit organization dedicated to effectively end animal cruelty and the inhumane methods of killing animals. I realize that I can't save every animal, but the fact that I can save at least a few is important to me. Some of my most satisfying days have been those when I helped find homes for abandoned cats that would have been eaten by coyotes in the wild. I have brought over twenty cats and kittens home to Denver from LaGrange and helped place them in wonderful homes. By standing up for what I believe, I have discovered the possibilities are endless. If I take action, I hope others will follow, and thus we can start a ripple effect. I think that by speaking out, giving my time, and believing in my cause, I can play a major role in protecting animals.

## A Sports Essay

We've already discussed avoiding certain cliché topics, and sports have great potential for both hyperbole and formulaic "life lessons," two things admission readers don't need. However, if sports—or anything else, for that matter—is meaningful to you, by all means, write about it. Just find that angle that makes it yours.

One of Eric's students, a young woman named Jordan, happens to be one of the top free-style skiers in the country. She travels all over the country, competes against Olympic athletes, and then she returns to school, picking up right where she left off. It'd be silly for her *not* to talk about sports, but it'd also be silly to talk about skiing the way every other knucklehead would. You might not ski, but you could probably write about it without even thinking, "I stood at the top of the hill, looking down the mountain at the crowd below. The wind whistled through the pines . . ."

Ignoring such stories, Jordan talked about a specific from that time:

---

I love Libby. No really, I do. If you were forced to spend six hours wandering the tiny town of Libby, Montana, while your coach watched a tow truck pull the rental van out of two feet of snow, you would too. This is what happens when my ski team decides to take a "short cut." You'd think the word alone would be enough of an omen. How many horror movies have you seen with either that or "wrong turn" in its plot description? Never mind that we had told the rental company we were driving to Idaho instead of British Columbia, or that the last time Team Summit took a "short cut" we ended up sleeping on the shoulder of a highway in a rental van, minus a minute piece of equipment: the transmission. At least the highway was on the map this time. If only we had seen the sign warning, "Road not maintained during winter." Even so, we probably should have clued ourselves in on that one when we saw the two-foot-high snow bank in the middle of the road. But, as always, that didn't stop us. What DID stop us was a shortage of gas and enough snow to drown a swim instructor. So, being logical human beings, we dialed 911 only to find that there was no cell signal. Anywhere. Finally, at eleven at night

my coach got just enough service to dial search and rescue, who eventually transported us to a hotel where the entire Libby Police Department
was waiting. (A forty-year-old man smuggling four female minors over
the border was the biggest news they'd had in years!) It was only after an
hour of questioning and long distance phone calls to our parents that they
finally let us rest. Fun, right?

Surprisingly, it was. Admittedly, telling ghost stories probably wasn't
the greatest comfort for four girls abandoned in the woods, but it somehow made the situation even more hilarious.

The unique quality of my life is that most of my significant experiences
happen in transit to my ever-varying activities. I'd like to think my music
education started in the car. Every time my dad and I had a four-hour
car ride from Aspen after another ski competition, he'd force me to listen
to "old people music," or worse: country. His favorite song to torment me
and my three siblings with was, and still is, "Amarillo by Morning." I'm half
embarrassed, half proud to say that I know every single word of that tor-
tuous song. I may have hated it at first, but now, I love it. I love it because
it reminds me of my dad's laugh or that simple fun of being playfully tor-
tured. Listening to that song was like being tickled. You hate it, you beg
for it to stop, and yet you're laughing the whole way through.

In situations like that, you have two options: gripe and moan, or make
it fun. Years of travelling as the rookie on my ski team has helped me
learn this. Being jammed into a seat that was clearly meant for a four-
year-old was hard at first, but after a while I figured out how to have a
good time all the same (that and your legs get numb). And hey, at the
very least, you're going to end up with a great story with a priceless "I love
Libby" bumper sticker as a reminder.

---

Jordan could have easily started off with a list of how many awards
she's won, but she didn't. Instead, she talked about a small town in
Montana and a funny song, both of which give us a real sense of who
she is.

### The Odd Question Essay

A number of schools want to see how creatively you respond to odd-
ball questions. (Imagine!) Cal Tech, for example, wants to make sure
that they're not getting all tunnel-vision math dudes, so one of their
"questions" in the past was, "Fill this box with something creative."

Several years ago, one of Eric's mathematically brilliant students
approached him with near terror in his eyes, "What am I supposed to
do with *this*?" he implored.

"Do you like being creative?" Eric asked him.

"Not really," the student said.

The student ended up not being accepted.

Another school known for its off-the-wall questions is the University of Chicago. One of our students, Andrew, responded to their "tell us about your table" prompt. And though we've seen students take essays like that and literally describe a table—in vivid detail, nonetheless—Andy decided to use the table as a stepping-off point for one of his primary extracurricular interests, speech and debate. Now, it'd be easy with an essay like this to forget about the table entirely and just talk about the interests and activities part, but Andy does a nice job balancing the two.

---

My table is a rectangle. It has the typical light brown wood found in many rooms in my school. It is meant for two people, allowing them to sit side by side. But just this one table alone isn't enough. It becomes my table under more specific circumstances.

My table exists in a converted art room in my school, where seven of these same tables have been arranged to form a larger rectangle with a pair of chairs facing inward at each of the seven tables. Many of these tables are covered in papers, highlighters, and pens. At most of the tables, there is one person working, and all together there are six people working (including me). The six people are the six senior debaters on my school's policy debate team, and the papers in front of them constitute debate evidence. It is under these conditions that one of these tables becomes mine.

The above described scene occurs many times during the school year. On any given day, the six of us will gather after school at these tables and work on debate arguments. While we are working, we feel free to bounce ideas off each other about a possible argument or to challenge an argument that someone is already working on.

Jesse, one debater, often tries to find a way to work in a nihilistic argument with supporting evidence from Nietzsche. Last year, he contemplated trying to win a debate in a nihilistic fashion by simply typing an argument, using Nietzsche as backup evidence and giving it to the judge at the beginning of the round. And while he wasn't serious about actually carrying out his plan, because it would likely have cost him the debate due to his lack of actually saying anything, we as a team found a way for him to argue that the government should not take action in a specific instance by using Nietzsche's logic. The idea landed on the table as a joke.

As we all passed it around like bread or gravy; it took shape, however. It came to life.

Jared, my debate partner, and I love to discuss securitization in our debates. Drawing upon David Campbell's logic in his book Writing Security and a few other authors' ideas, we have argued many times that the United States should not take action in certain international situations in the name of eliminating artificially constructed threats. It was at the "discussion tables," however, that we wrote the argument and then developed it by hearing how our teammates would argue against it.

Jordan, another debater, often provides an interesting perspective, using Foucault's writings about biopower. She uses his arguments to state that we as citizens should or shouldn't take action against a certain policy based on whether or not it gives too much power to the government. Of course, before she argues it in a debate round, she brings it to the table and tests it against the rest of us.

The discussions at these tables have taught me a lot. I have learned about different philosophers' and thinkers' arguments. Beyond that, I have learned to defend ideas by discussing them with five very intelligent and knowledgeable people. I have discovered that, in the realm of intellectual thought, any argument or approach is worth trying. I have also learned that when developing that argument or thought, an intellectual community can be the most valuable tool I have.

---

Even though he might have spent a bit too much time amplifying this one component of his activity roster, the table nonetheless gave Andy the chance to talk about one of his primary loves—debate.

## THE SUPPLEMENTS

With all these essays, it might be easy to forget something that's just as important: the supplement. Remember these little guys? As we mentioned before, some schools even use these as the real litmus test for the sort of writer a student is because students don't usually spend as much time polishing these.

A common supplement question is why do you want to come to our school? (Remember, this is where we told you to be as detailed as you can. Colleges are tired of reading about the "great classes" and "beautiful campus" in these mini-essays. Also, such comments show that you haven't really done your research.)

There are many other supplement questions, though, and we've provided two below, both of which come from a thoughtful student-athlete named Dylan. The first prompt is, "talk about a person who has influenced you," and the second asks that the student respond to a William James quotation.

Dylan does a great job with these two pieces because just as the other students did with their full essays, Dylan also does here: He gives us a tangible, personal view of his world. Beyond his clean writing style, we have a real sense of the sort of person he is and where he comes from—details that don't necessarily appear on the regular application.

### Person Who Has Influenced Me

I don't have to look far to find the person who has influenced me the most in my life. He has shown me where true grit and humility can take you. Let me introduce you to my father, Asdrubal José "Joe" Solarte.

Born in Cali, Colombia, my father was the eldest of four children. Buoyed by the promise of a better life in America, his mother was the first to immigrate to an affluent suburb of Chicago to work as a live-in nanny. Over several years, she worked to become financially stable to send for each of her children. It was my father who was the last of the four to arrive in America in 1970. Unable to speak English and with no opportunities to learn how, he was mainstreamed into a public middle school and began his life as "Yo Solarte." After struggling through all the ups and downs of middle school myself, I can't even imagine what guts he must have had to live as an immigrant in an affluent suburb of Chicago.

My grandmother continued to struggle to support her family alone, but she also relied on my father to help pay for groceries. After school, instead of heading off to soccer practice as I have for many years, my father walked to the nearby country club to wash dishes. There are times when I've been frustrated with hand-me-downs and less-than-glamorous camping trips with our family of eight, but I have never gone without what I need, and I have my father to thank for that.

My father went on to attend the University of Wisconsin-Madison and was able to play on their Varsity Soccer team. He became a commercial real estate broker and is proud of his large family of six. Although at times he works three jobs to give us every opportunity to excel on the soccer field and in the classroom, he never complains. I think sometimes he thrives on hard work, but I still hope someday that I can afford to send both of my parents on a much needed vacation.

Although my father's childhood was filled with challenges I've never had to face, his fortitude has given me a clear sense of what is important. He is quick to remind me that "all you need in life is one ironed shirt, a good work ethic, and the best education you can afford." I'm hoping that I can prove to my father that his desire for a better life for himself and his family made real sense.

### "The art of being wise is knowing what to overlook." from "The Principles of Psychology" (1890) by William James

Have you ever traveled with eight people (one of whom was throwing up into a salad spinner) on a family vacation in a packed Suburban, pulling a pop-up camper? Well, I have, and I'm telling you, you have to be mighty wise to realize that just about everything that happens in a big family must be overlooked.

Take chores, for example. As the oldest of six, I have been forced to complete chores with the biggest group of underachievers I've ever met—my siblings. I have a younger brother, Greer, whose best attribute is how to get OUT of work. When it's time to clean the kitchen, he suddenly has the strongest urge to go to the bathroom for 30 minutes. By the time he's out of bathroom, the job is done. When he does work, his work is below par. He forgets to wipe down the table or the counters after dinner and after he's gone to bed, I'm the one to finish his job. Living in a big family means that you have to be able to look past the little, annoying things that everyone you live with does and focus more on the big picture.

I've learned that as you take a deep breath and overlook your siblings' faults, it might just come in handy in other situations as well. I realized this recently with one of my friends at school. I lent my Spanish vocabulary book to a friend for a night. But when I asked for it back the next day, he said that he had lost it and that he was so sorry. Although I was pretty angry, I knew that he was going through some rough times in his life so I said it was fine and that I would just find another person's book and make copies of the lessons. By applying some of the life lessons I learn at home to my everyday life, I saved this friendship, and I now consider him to be one of my best friends.

My life at home is never glamorous like the lives of so many of my friends at school, but by learning to overlook some of the worst parts of living in a big family, life at home can actually be quite enjoyable. I have to say I've had fun playing Monopoly for days at a time, playing soccer in the living room, and sleeping in blanket forts we put together with anything we could find. Sometimes I come home from soccer, and the house is empty, and I don't know where everyone is. It's strange for my house to be so quiet. So I usually call one of my parents and ask, "Where is everyone?"

That's why I think that when I go to college, I'll miss the noise. Hopefully, though, dorm life will afford me another opportunity to practice the wisdom I've learned living in a family of eight.

## THE PHOTO

Should you send one? Most applicants don't, and it's rarely—if ever—required, but a handful of schools such as the University of Pennsylvania ask for a mug shot as an optional part of the application. If you want to send one, even to a college that doesn't ask, it likely won't hurt, but keep it simple. Don't send a "Glamour Shot" taken in the mall, a family picture, or you posing in your cheerleading outfit. A simple, straightforward headshot is all you'd need. Why is it not a bad thing? When the admission rep is wading through stacks of papers, it's nice to have a face to associate with a GPA and an ACT score.

Now, it's worth pointing out that more universities might ask for the photo were it not for the rather insidious history connected to it. In *The Chosen: The Hidden History of Admission and Exclusion at Harvard, Yale, and Princeton*, the author, Jerome Karabel, says that Harvard began asking for photos in the 1920's to discriminate against Jewish candidates more efficiently. In today's world, however, a photo might actually help a school create a more diverse student body.

How times change.

---

### Fragment from Napoleon's Love Letter to Josephine:

"Indeed, I am very uneasy, my love, at receiving no news of you; write me quickly four pages, pages full of agreeable things which shall fill my heart with the pleasantest feelings. I hope before long to crush you in my arms and cover you with a million kisses burning as though beneath the equator."

(Now *that's* hot writing!)

## Chapter 10

# How to Play the Game

Diversity, athletics, legacy, first-generation college, development office candidacy...

*"All that matters is love and work."*

—FREUD

The college admission process is an entirely fair competition, and each school wants the smartest, most talented, most accomplished, most well-rounded student, correct? Wrong. First, keep in mind that most schools don't care so much about the well-rounded student. They prefer, rather, a well-rounded class. So if this means accepting a cook from Des Moines over a race-car driver from Greensboro, so be it. At this stage in the game, after you've done your best in every way, it's not about you. It's about them.

President George W, when talking recently about affirmative action, suggested that school admission should ideally be fair and equal to all, with "ideally" being the operative word. It seems he'd forgotten that he had been the recipient of a different sort of affirmative action—that afforded wealthy legacy families. Based on grades and high school performance, there's no way George W would have been admitted to Yale. Ever.

So, now we talk about some of the many caveats in the college admission world. All this is to remind you that you shouldn't feel so bad if things don't turn out in your favor. There are forces at work, some well-intentioned, others less so, that are out of your control. (And we're talking about college admission now and dating, too, believe it or not.)

1) **Diversity.** One of the most important aspects of college is that it introduces students to new ideas—not just in the classroom, but outside, too, and much of this newness is a direct result of diversity. Most high schools are fairly homogeneous places, but colleges tend to be institutions that strive for various types of diversity—economic, social, religious, and ethnic. Even colleges fumble, though. Often, "diversity" becomes a catch word that refers exclusively to race—or, more specifically, the diversity we can see. When visiting an elite college not long ago, another counselor asked the admission director the following question: "If you had to choose between an African-American student from a high school in inner-city Chicago, or an African-American student who'd attended a well-to-do independent school in the Northeast, who would you pick?" At first, the director said, "The inner-city student, of course," but then, after pondering a few seconds longer, the officer was honest enough to share the following, "But the reality is, we'd probably end up accepting the student from the independent school. Simply, he 'looks' diverse, but we likely wouldn't have to spend lots of money on him or organize a whole support system of tutors and such. It's unfortunate, but true." On a related note, if you have some ethnic background you want to declare on an application, make sure it's real and meaningful to you. If you're one of the many kids with "some" Native American blood running in your veins, that's all fine and good, but don't say

it on the college app unless you've actually got proof that you're affiliated with a tribe. The college may very well ask.

2) **Sports.** We all know the stereotype that athletes get preferential treatment over regular students—both pre and post admission. Although the reports of much of this treatment have been blown out of proportion, it still exists. At Division I schools, coaches are allowed a certain number of spaces for their teams. Obviously, if a kid is a real super-star on the field or the court, academics might get brushed aside. The coach still prefers a good student, though, because it makes his conversation with the admission office that much easier. A word to all would-be athletes, though: be careful with coaches. Most are nice, well-meaning people, but for one reason or another, they often make promises that the admission office can't keep. A 2007 *New York Times* article noted how squash and crew have recently been "discovered" as a back door into many of the selective universities. Maybe this is true, but it's still a back door that's now been found out—with the moral being, don't force yourself to play squash if you don't really like it.

### So . . . Think You Wanna Play, Do You?

A) Go to www.ncaa.org

B) Talk to your high school coach to see if his or her assessment of your abilities is similar to yours.

C) Write to college coaches.

D) Give contact info for college coaches to your high school coach.

E) Before a visit to a college, schedule appointments with coaches.

F) Do a camp or two over the summer that college coaches will visit.

3) **Legacy.** This refers to the family connection to a school, and while it doesn't matter one jot at some places, others put it at a premium.

4) **Moolah.** The simple fact of the matter is that, alas, money can buy a lot more than you'd think. The nicer term for this would be "development office prospect," but if a college has a building with

your grandfather's name on it, you're pretty much set to go there. One father, when called by his alma mater for a routine-type donation, asked, "Will this help my son get in?" to which the caller responded with a, "Not really." The father, not skipping a beat, said, "Then I'm not giving you a donation." The kid, obviously, didn't get in.

5) **Your High School.** Though independent high schools typically provide more guidance both in academics and during the college counseling process, don't despair if you attend a big public high school. Remember: colleges want diversity, and your being from a public high school could be part of that very equation. Also, colleges are aware that not every high school is equal, so they want to see that you've attempted to max out all the opportunities you could, wherever you are. If your high school only offers up to French III, did you meet with the French teacher for personal tutoring sessions after you completed that level?

6) **Your State.** Even this counts as diversity. Colleges like to brag about how many states are represented in their student body. So while you can't be a dimwit from North Dakota and be admitted into Amherst, if you're a smart guy from Alaska, you'll have a much better shot than another smart guy from Massachusetts. Lynda credits her Stanford acceptance at least partly to her being from New Mexico.

7) **First Generation College Student.** If you're the first in your family to go to college, that's a real plus. (So you can tell the legacies to "take that.") Lynda had this one going for her, too, by the way.

## BEHIND THE CLOSED DOORS OF AN ADMISSION OFFICE

Considering all this, let's look at what really goes on behind the closed doors of an admission office.

The slam-dunk kids get in right away, and the Bland Betties get dropped pretty fast. But what happens to all those mid-range kids—the majority—who don't have some hugely obvious "hook"? Simple: they end up going to committee, which is where all the mystery (according to outsiders, at least) takes place.

If you're curious to know what goes on, it's pretty straightforward. Here's a run-down from a typical small, liberal arts college.

First, every application is read by three people. That part of the process tends to go pretty quickly. Then, one person reads aloud a sort of *Cliff's Notes* version of the kid's file while the others follow along with their own notes, listening. Occasionally, the director or dean asks a pointed question, such as, "any reason to admit this kid?" or, if the candidate sounds good, "any flies on this one?" after which the folder would find itself plopped in the appropriate pile—admit, reject, or wait list.

We mentioned that the high school you attend plays into your chances of admission. To determine a high school's rank—which is something that a number of colleges do—a college creates a formula based on the percentage of students going on to college calculated in with the school's average SAT scores. Often, the colleges use a scale of 1 to 5.

A breakdown of a kid's application looks something like this: GPA, rigor of course load, SAT or ACT, family "situation" (where sibling[s] or other family members attended college, parents' jobs, special circumstances, etc.), why the student is interested in the first place, activities, academic and personal rankings, course summary, a snapshot version of teacher recs, and a synopsis of writing samples—usually only one or two lines. (Typically, these say something like: "Tells story of growing up in small town. Pros and cons. Vivid prose. Really brings to life.")

Odd and interesting acronyms crop up. Curious to know what a DOA is? At some schools, it's a "Daughter of Alum." How about SS? Why, "Sport-Soccer," of course. And PQ? Try "Personal Qualities."

Amid all these abbreviations and summaries, most admission people genuinely want to sense the person behind the numbers, and they love it when you give them something to latch on to—something interesting and compelling.

Before we wrap up this section, we should add a little disclaimer. All this talk of "playing the game" can be misleading. Some get so caught up in the competitive aspects of it all, they blur the ethical line. We've already talked about professionals who help "polish"—ghost write, essentially—student essays, but there are other examples, too. In the March 14, 2005 *The New York Times* article "Not Yet In Business

School, and Already Flunking Ethics," journalist Tom Zeller tells the story. As he says, "eager business school applicants—most of them aiming at Harvard—exploited a technical glitch to get an early peek at their pending decisions online." Basically, a student had posted directions on how to sneak an early look at acceptances (as well as rejections), and 119 Harvard applicants did. Zaller wrote that almost 100 applicants to other business schools at MIT, Carnegie Mellon, Stanford, Dartmouth, and Duke used the instructions as well. Arguments for each side exploded on the Internet. Though the 119 students were rejected for the ethical breach and welcome to reapply the following year, for many that wasn't enough. They thought they hadn't done anything wrong. The moral of this story is that, with this world of information exchange on the Web, some ethical decisions become ever murkier. If you're even a little unsure about a decision you're about to make—whether it involves an application or a project at school—err on the conservative side.

### Attractive Body Language

1) Tilt your head when listening.

2) Keep your stance open, arms out rather than crossed.

3) If you want to see if someone's checking you out, glance at your watch; then see if that person does, too.

4) Be expressive but not spastic.

5) Flash your pearly whites.

6) Cover your mouth when belching.

# Paying for Dinner

### Financial aid and scholarships

> *"The love of money and the love of learning rarely meet."*
> —GEORGE HERBERT

We've all been there. You're in a restaurant, and the meal is over. You're happy with how this first date has gone, but then you reach for your wallet and . . . it's gone! So you have your date sneak out the bathroom window, but then you get caught and you're thrown in jail for . . .

Wait. Maybe that's not *everyone's* experience.

Just so no one's left looking for the missing wallet, make sure you and your parents talk about finances from the start. You don't want to put an undue burden on them, but they want to make sure you're happy, too.

College is expensive. Even if you attend your local state school and live at home, it's going to cost you and your family plenty. If you're one of the lucky few who don't have to worry about the price of higher education, just skip this chapter and save your brain cells for other purposes—like deciding who to invite to prom.

For the rest of you, we'd advise marshalling your frontal cortex into top working order. Financial aid is complicated, inconsistent, and confusing—just like so many aspects of this process and so much like the quest for true love. We'll first give you an overview of how this part of the puzzle works, then some suggestions to follow, and finally, a few stories.

Basically, there are two types of financial aid: There's need-based aid, where students are awarded money based on the family's demonstrated need, and there's merit-based aid, which we like to call "please come" money. The former is given to the neediest students based on various forms that they and their parents fill out. The latter is awarded to students with particular gifts—intellectual, athletic, or otherwise, in an attempt to lure them to a college that really wants them. Sometimes a student who is both needy and talented will receive both kinds of aid.

## THE THREE BASIC CATEGORIES OF AID MONEY

1) **Scholarships/Grants**—This is free money that doesn't have to be repaid, ever. Obviously, this is preferable to any other kind. Some need-based aid falls under this heading, and merit-based aid is always free money. The best scholarships in most cases come directly through the college. There are a few good ones that you can apply for on your own, but generally, if you're lucky enough to win that outside scholarship, any scholarship funds you're awarded by your college will be reduced correspondingly. If you land a really huge one, great! It's worth it. Unfortunately, those really big outside scholarships have applications that take a lot of time and effort. We've seen very worthy students work super-hard and come up with nothing from some of the major ones like those sponsored by Coca-Cola and Toyota. By the way, take the hype about "millions of dollars of aid going unclaimed" as just one more bit of chicanery associated with this process. There are all sorts of unscrupulous individuals and agencies out there

offering to "help"—for a fee. They're generally just out to help themselves.

2) **Loans—**These have to be repaid after graduation. You and your parents may be aware of the scandals recently uncovered about the whole student loan business. The best loans come from your favorite uncle, Uncle Sam. The rates will be lower than private loans, and the terms will be more humane. Make sure you know exactly what you're getting into before you take out any type of student loan; shop around for rates and terms that you and your parents can live with!

3) **Work-study—**These are jobs that the college gives students as part of their aid package. Because they come from the financial aid office at the college, they fit in with your schedule for classes and recognize that you need time to do your homework.

Some of those same factors that make students attractive candidates when they apply for admission can make them attractive in the financial aid process. Wealthier colleges have more money to spend on aid than do the others. Some of the richest, Princeton and Davidson among them, have completely done away with student loans. All the money they award comes in the form of scholarships—that is, free money. Quite a few other "elite" colleges, like U. Chicago, Northwestern, Columbia, and Harvard, have eliminated loans, giving grants instead to students whose family incomes fall below a certain level. Interestingly, because some of these schools don't really need to lure talented students, all their aid is strictly need-based. Also interestingly, some colleges with less-fat endowments will go all out to try to win a particularly appealing candidate, sometimes offering a scholarship that amounts to discounting tuition and sometimes offering a full ride—even when there's no need involved! To receive this kind of royal treatment, you'll need to have grades, scores, and other qualifications that will make you a much-desired candidate.

## A FEW SUGGESTIONS

1) Figure out which forms each of your colleges requires for financial aid. Anyone applying for need-based aid will have to do the

FAFSA (all the information is available at www.fafsa.ed.gov), and from there on, it's a real mish-mash. Some colleges require the PROFILE, another basic form; others will require their own forms; and yet others will want them all. To further complicate matters, there are more and different forms for loans. Ask the lenders to help you understand them. The financial aid offices at the colleges are generally very helpful when you or your parents have questions about paperwork. To gauge what your FAFSA might be before you're able to apply in January, check www.fafsa4caster.com.

2) Your family and you can get an idea regarding your need-based aid eligibility by going to www.collegeboard.com and working with the College Board's Expected Family Contribution (EFC) calculator.

3) As you apply, try to find out if each college is "need blind" or simply "need sensitive." The former do not take into account whether or not you'll need aid in order to attend. The latter may actually reject needy students who might be accepted if they were full-pay. That brings us to a practice called "gapping." When a school "gaps" a student, it accepts that student but does not offer a package that meets all demonstrated need. Their thinking is that the student and her family may be able to come up with the extra cash—maybe by borrowing from rich relatives or winning the lottery. Obviously, if your family isn't likely to qualify for need-based aid, don't apply for it. As a full-pay, you may be a more desirable candidate. Once you're in, you can apply for aid for your sophomore year. Outstanding freshman-year grades will be an asset if you decide to do this.

4) If you qualify for need-based aid, it's a good idea to compare aid packages from all the schools that admit you. To do this effectively, you can't apply early decision because you need to see all the information about each school's offer side by side. That's not only the total amount, but also the break-down: How much is grant (free) money? How much is loan? How much is work study? Look closely and ask questions. See what the real costs to you and your family will be. One of Lynda's advisees received almost identical offers from two colleges he really liked. What tipped the

scale in favor of one over the other? It was the *type* of work-study involved; one college had a great community-service job for him, while the other offered only custodial work. Sit down with your parents once you have all the acceptances and offers in hand, and look at what's what. You may be surprised. It's not unusual to find that attending a private school that really wants you, although the tuition there is higher, will cost less than going to the local state university where there's lower tuition.

5) If you're wait-listed at a school where you could only attend if you received financial aid, you probably should forget about that one. Even if you were accepted later on, the aid money would most likely be all gone by then.

6) Beware of scams. It seems to us as if the neediest families are targeted with the most dishonest offers. All too often, students bring in letters about "seminars" that they and their parents are invited to attend. For only a few hundred dollars, the letters promise, undiscovered scholarship dollars will fly directly into their hands. If a scholarship offer seems too good to be true, it probably is—except when it comes directly from the college, of course!

7) State schools will have lower tuition rates, but some of the small liberal arts colleges will have more money to offer.

8) Ask about aid consortia or reciprocal tuition discounts among states. For example, Colorado is part of WICHE (the Western Interstate Commission on Higher Education), which offers reduced tuition exchanges with several other states.

## PLAYING THE FINANCIAL AID GAME—A FEW STORIES

Close to home, Lynda, whose family qualified for need-based aid, was lucky enough to attend college with an aid package that consisted of both a university scholarship and a government loan. In the evenings, she worked at the student health service. Lynda's sister, coming from the same needy family, attended a less "prestigious" institution that was very glad to net a student of her intellectual gifts. As a result, her sister received a no-loan, no-work package consisting of both need-based and merit-based aid. Lynda, as you'd guess, didn't finish paying off her loans—even though the terms were generous and the interest low—until she was thirty-five. She has always considered that money a good investment, but even still . . . thirty-five?

Remember how we said that the best scholarships generally come through the college's financial aid office? Well, a few years ago, Lynda had an advisee who was brilliant, talented, and noble. She made top grades in the toughest courses, played varsity sports expertly, and worked 40 hours a week to support her dying father and herself. No kidding. As part of applying to college, she also applied for all sorts of big-time scholarships, 45 of them, to be precise. How many of those did she win? That's right—none, nada, zero. The good news is that she attended Rice University on full aid.

Another of Lynda's advisees, this one more recent, found herself in financial aid trouble just before May 1 when she had to make a decision between two very good colleges. The difficulty came when her parents didn't qualify for a loan that was considered part of the package at both schools. Heroically, Lake Forest College came through with an alternate university loan that was made only to the student, not her parents. Surely, we don't have to tell you where she's studying.

One of our students was a guy with a story that spoke of heart, courage, brains, and spirit. He'd attended elementary school in a one-room building with no books in a tiny village in the Dominican Republic, moved to Denver without knowing any English, and worked through Kent Denver's college prep curriculum, earning a solid B average. He was courted by several excellent schools, but he needed aid, lots of it, and he spent many hours applying for quite a few scholarships. Once he'd won a good one, we checked with the colleges where he was accepted to find out what this seeming good fortune would do to his aid package. If you've been keeping up, you probably know that his grant money would be reduced by the amount of his outside scholarship. In short, he had been spending all that time to help the colleges' budgets, and doing little to benefit himself. Once he understood that interesting fact, he stopped applying for more scholarships and focused on catching up in his classes and studying for final exams.

What happens when a super-attractive candidate, say a bright, capable student of color who has established an excellent record receives the least appealing aid package from her first-choice college? That was the situation for one of Lynda's African-American advisees. The student, Aphrodite, made a chart detailing how much of each offer from her three top-choice schools was grant, loan, and work-study so that she could compare real costs. Murphy's law was no doubt at work: the college where the weather was coldest and the student body least diverse—and not her favorite—gave her the most free money, resulting in the lowest overall cost. Aphrodite brought her mother to school for a pow-wow. Lynda counseled the mother to call the favorite college, the one offering the least grant money, and lay her cards on the table. After the mom had explained that her daughter wouldn't be able to attend because the financial aid offers were so much better at both of the other contenders, the financial aid officer at true-love college was able to revise the package so that everyone was happy. Aphrodite got to study where she most wanted to, the college got a fabulous young woman who will do great things, and the family got the aid that made it all possible.

As a bit of good news, in 2003, the wealthier schools began offering aggressive aid programs for their poorest students. Then, in 2007, with Congress pushing these well-off institutions to spend more of their endowments, many began offering improved packages to middle and upper-middle class families, too. Though true socio-economic diversity is still a way off, and we're not quite a meritocracy yet, there is definitely movement in the right direction. For two shining examples of what this direction might look like, check out Berea College and Cooper Union, two schools that are free to their students.

### Cheap Dates

1) Make tacos together.

2) Stargaze.

3) Visit a museum on its free night.

4) People-watch at the mall.

5) Have fun at a playground—without scaring the little kids.

6) Volunteer together.

7) Take a walk in the park.

8) Study for a test together.

9) Help each other babysit.

10) Re-enact the Obi Wan vs. Darth Vader light saber scene.

Chapter 12

# The Wait
## Waiting for an answer

*"All things come to those who wait."*
—16TH CENTURY PROVERB

Y ou might have heard the rule about not calling for two days after the first date so you don't seem desperate. Others say you should call whenever you feel like it because, hey, you're being yourself. College admission "rules" for waiting are just about as hazy.

So now, you've sent everything off into the vast beyond. Your applications have gone, along with the magnum opus of an essay, supplements, rec letters . . . now you can relax, right? Right?? Wrong. Now you'll sit, looking at the clock and calendar, staring as the seconds, minutes, hours, days, and weeks tick by, wondering if things got lost in the mail or cyberspace, wondering if you said the right thing in the essay, wondering if The College Board really sent your scores and not some other kid's who never spent all those hours doing practice tests at the kitchen table.

You really should take a deep breath. If the college is missing something, the admission office will send you a notification saying so. Don't be alarmed if you receive a postcard or email saying you didn't send something when you know you did. Often, with the amount of paper-work admission offices receive, there's a normal delay in processing. Many times, students have called to learn that yes, the transcript did, in fact, arrive. If the college still insists that it didn't receive anything, don't worry about this either: the folks there know this happens. (And, though you don't need to say this to them, more often than not, the item was lost in the mix right at the admission office.) Find out what the missing item is, politely express your concern since you did send it, and then let them know you'll be sending along a copy immediately. You *did* keep that copy we talked about, didn't you?

While you wait, remember a few things:

1) Stay in touch with the colleges you've applied to. Remember, with the Common App and electronic applications, it's easy to apply to too many schools. How will a college know whether you're really interested or just applying there "in case . . ."? One of Lynda's advisees, a sweet, bright girl who was a terrific student and an excellent writer, applied early to a very long shot and regular decision to a few good, small liberal arts colleges—all good matches. After she was deferred by Fancy-Pants U, she figured that her targets would work out. She was a well qualified applicant for all of them, despite her rather modest standardized-test scores. Then came the first week in April. The news was not good; she was accepted at only one school and wait-listed at another. Lynda called a friend in the admission office of the college where her advisee was wait-listed to ask what the deal was. The informative reply was that because the student had never visited, never done the optional interview, never introduced herself to the rep, and never even phoned or emailed to ask a question, that the admission office assumed the girl was not really interested in the school. Lynda knew otherwise, but it was too late. The student had feared seeming too pushy and hoped that her application would speak for itself.

On the opposite end of the spectrum, another of Lynda's advisees, a young man with great personal charm and only reasonable grades and scores, never missed an opportunity to make contact with his colleges. He sought out the reps at fairs, made sure to remember their names, wrote thank-you notes after visits and interviews, and generally made a positive—and lasting—impression on everyone he met. Even so, we were pleasantly surprised when he was admitted to his first-choice college. Interestingly, the rep from his most impossible, longest-shot school told Lynda that although there was no way the student could be admitted there, he thought he'd be a great guy to hang out with. (Whatever, right?)

2) There's a difference between staying in touch and making ridiculous overtures in an attempt to win over the admission office. The personal note to the officer you met with during your visit is a great idea. But gifts? Not so much.

Admission reps have told us crazy stories about things applicants have sent in an attempt to make an impression. One student sent a cake with his face on it. "We were at the point of admitting him," the rep explained, "until the cake came . . . then we just couldn't." Another student sent a box of balloons with (yep, get ready for another face story) her grinning mug on each. "By the end of the week, we had all these half-deflated balloons with this girl's crumpled face floating around the office, and it was just sad. It sort of reminded us of her deflated hopes." Then there was the kid from the steamy south who mailed an air conditioner—that's right, a whole air conditioner—to Stanford's admission office, explaining that he wouldn't need it in Palo Alto's perfect climate. Needless to say, he'd have been better off keeping his cooler! Many stalkers and creepoids think they're "in love" and that they just need to convince the other person. In relationships or in college admission, persistence might pay off sometimes, but obsessive clinginess never does.

3) Keep up with your activities and your sports. Have fun with your friends and family. Have a life!

4) DO NOT come down with the dreaded "senioritis." As a senior, you might feel like you've earned some down time. You haven't. You're still a kid. "Senioritis" should belong to those seventy and older. But here's the scenario: a student will receive an acceptance from any one of the colleges she's applied to, and suddenly, she acts as if nothing else matters. School's over; she's finished.

Cruise control from there on out. But hold on. Because of the increased levels of competition, colleges are keeping a closer eye on their admits than ever before. Every year, a student or two in our senior class will receive a letter explaining that the university is sad to notice that so-and-so's grades have dropped, and that, for the first semester, the student will be placed on . . . (gulp) . . . academic probation. Every now and again, an acceptance will actually be rescinded. The point is, while you may be able to relax a little more once things are sent, you're still a student, and going to high school is still your job.

### How to Know if You're a Stalker

1) You've called the person ten times. In an hour.

2) You think it's romantic to show up, unannounced, late at night at the person's house.

3) You think the neighbor in *Disturbia* is sort of cool.

4) You don't have time to read books like this because you're too busy looking up information about the person online.

## Chapter 13

# Mixed Messages— The Wait List

What you can do if it happens to you

*"Hunger I can endure; love I cannot."*
—CLAUDIAN

So, you've received an answer. If it's "yes," then blow up the balloons, toss the confetti, and celebrate! If you received acceptances from several of the colleges on your list, then you have been presented with the delightful dilemma of choosing among them. Remember, you only applied to schools you'd like to attend! We'll talk more about these choices in Chapter 16. If you got that skinny envelope saying "no," that's pretty clear, too. We'll talk more about that in the next chapter. The confusing answer is the "we want you, sort of" one—you've been placed on the wait list. What does this mean?

Every college has a different approach to the wait list, and that approach changes from year to year. Admission offices have to do a lot of fancy math to predict who will actually be enrolling each year. If too many admitted students attend (that is, the college gets a higher "yield" than it predicted), there won't be enough space in the dorms. We remember one year when The University of Richmond was so popular that upper classmen were moved off campus to make room for all the new freshmen, and another year, Colorado College put freshmen in nearby motels for lack of space on campus. If, on the other hand, not enough admitted students enroll (the "yield" is lower than predicted), the college is stuck with a budget crisis unless it can drum up more students. This isn't so hot for on-campus morale, either. These days, with students applying to ever-greater numbers of colleges and the colleges not knowing where they stand on the students' lists, admission offices often accept a minimal number of students and create a long wait list, figuring that they have a safety net.

That safety net can become really important when there are big changes in the admission world such as some of the hottest colleges' (Harvard, Princeton, and UVA, among others) getting rid of their early admission programs. As an example, let's take a look at what happened in May of 2008. Before then, Harvard and other colleges of that ilk had always been reasonably certain about what their yield would look like. Here's why: Even an early action program works well in terms of getting students' minds set on a certain college. It's basic psychology: if you're admitted to a very cool place in December, even in a non-binding program, you start thinking in terms of going there. Students already enrolled at the college who have something in common with you (ethnicity, major, musical talent . . . you get the idea) are phoning and emailing you, telling you how great the new theater is or what a terrific time they had at the campus in Barcelona. You start to *see* yourself there, and you're feeling pretty committed. Take away that early piece, and applicants are waiting until late March or early April to find out what their choices are. In 2008, a side effect was that yields went awry, and all those projections and calculations that the number-crunchers in the admission offices had done were not always so accurate. Harvard announced it would offer admission to an unprecedented 150-175 students on its waiting list. This created a domino effect on other colleges' new admits because, and we're being hypothetical, a kid who deposited on May 1 to, say, Bowdoin, decided to accept Harvard's offer to come off the wait list. That left a space in Bowdoin's new freshman class, so Bowdoin's admission office then dipped into its wait list, taking a student from another college a little lower on the food chain, adding more chaos to an already confusing process.

So, in sum, the wait list provides a cushion for the college if not enough of the accepted students accept the college's acceptances and enroll. Make sense? ***The wait list exists to help the college, not to help you.*** We've seen students who don't understand this get all excited about a school that wait-lists them. Suddenly, there's the allure of the "club" that *might* have you as a member. Somehow, that college can seem more exciting than the ones where you're welcomed. This goes back to that whole thing about human nature—we want what we don't have.

Now that you have all this background, what do you do if a college that genuinely interests you puts you on the wait list? There are no guarantees, of course, and the colleges generally don't have any real sense of how they'll use their wait lists until the first week in May when they've heard back from the students they've admitted. But here are the tactics you should use if you want to try to move off the wait list and gain acceptance:

1) Send that postcard saying that you want to remain on the wait list—but this is only the first step.

2) You avoided senioritis, right? So send your most recent report card with those good grades you're still earning.

3) Ask your counselor and/or a teacher to write an additional note for you, describing something you've done since submitting your application. Did you write a great editorial for the newspaper last month? How about that research paper for AP Chem, the one your teacher said was the best in the class? Was your performance in the spring musical a show stopper?

4) Write your own letter, briefly outlining any awards you've gotten, honors bestowed on you, the championship your team won, or any other recent accomplishments and activities that will strengthen your case. Now comes the biggie, the thing that can make all the difference on that wait list (assuming the school is

using it at all): Promise you'll come if you're accepted. Of course, you can only do this if it's TRUE. Think long and hard before making this promise.

5) As we said in the last chapter, remember the difference between showing interest and stalking. Admission officers have told us that students who contact them sometimes are the ones accepted, and why? The "squeaky wheel" is also the wheel that'll end up attending if accepted, and colleges would obviously rather accept the students they know will come.

6) Find out if the school does mid-year admits, and if so, let them know you'd be willing to explore that as a possibility. Some universities stagger their freshman class, with students matriculating in the fall, winter, and sometimes even summer. Since most students prefer the idea of the traditional fall enrollment, this could give you a little nudge.

Here are a few more things to think about in connection with the wait list:

- Set a time in your own mind when you give up. How comfortable would you be if you were uncertain in July about where you're attending college? Wait lists can work like those little puzzles where you slide numbers around. There can be movement well into the summer as students change colleges when space opens up on their respective wait lists.

- Know that you probably won't have much of a choice about housing. The regular admits got to make their choices, and you'll be stuck with whatever is left over.

- If you need money, this will make a difference. The college has already assigned all the aid it has. Maybe a student with need won't even come off the wait list, but if she does, there won't be any funds available.

## How You Know If the Other Person Isn't That into You: S/He

1) Throws up uncontrollably every time you walk by

2) Lights his/her hair on fire when you say hello

3) Refuses to pay the ransom when you've been kidnapped

## Chapter 14

# Dealing with the Hurt

## Rejection

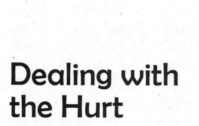

*"Man can be destroyed but not defeated."*
—ERNEST HEMINGWAY

We've all been there. If you haven't, you haven't really lived. We're talking, of course, about rejection. "Winning," we hear, "isn't what builds character. It's the losing that does it." The same holds true for being rejected.

Years ago, when a friend of Eric's was worried about how he had come across during a particularly lousy interchange with a woman, another friend looked over and explained, "She's not rejecting *you*; she's rejecting the situation." This sounds like bunk, but it's true. She didn't know Eric's friend. She only knew the situation. Now, had the guy looked a little more like George Clooney, she might have been a little more open to accepting the situation, but that's neither here nor there.

It's important to remember this same advice during the college process. It really and truly isn't all about you (though you'd like to think it
is). Remember in chapter 10 when we talked about how schools want a
well-rounded class more than a well-rounded person? Can you help it
if the college to which you're applying happened not to have a yodeler
from Indiana? They wanted that yodeler, *needed* that yodeler, but their
lack of yodelers and the fact that they admitted him instead of you
doesn't mean that you're not smart enough, good-looking enough, or
nice enough. Remember Don Juan from chapter two and how bad he'd
felt, even though he'd actually been accepted into the school he really
wanted? We've even seen kids later selected as Presidential Scholars
get rejected by schools, because—who knows?—maybe those schools
already had a potential Presidential Scholar from the Rocky Mountain
area.

**Unlike in relationships, then, when schools say, "It's not you;
it's me," they usually mean it. Yale, for example, recently said that
it figured at least 85% of its applicants could do the work.** With
that said, it's tough not to turn this thing into a tool for self-valida-
tion, but all we can say is *don't*. It's not worth your time or effort. Just
as you'll get rejected on the dating scene (and, if you never do, you
need to write a book of your own), you can't turn those rejections into
personal assessments of who you are. After all, why would you want to
"convince" a school that they should accept you if that college doesn't
see the fabulous qualities you have to offer? Similarly, why desperately
try to go out with someone who won't give you the time of day?

Here's the deal: you're better than that. This isn't a Mr. Rogers'
line. It's true. If you feel the need to twist someone's arm, either in the
college or dating world, to convince them that you've got a lot going
for you, then it's probably not worth the effort.

But doesn't a rejection from a college mean that you don't "have
what it takes" in life? Hardly!

In his book *Emotional Intelligence*, Daniel Goleman writes about one
of the true indicators of success in life, and it is, simply, the ability to
suck it up and take defeat with a smile. Essentially, his study revealed
how a special group of insurance sales people, chosen exclusively for
their optimism, outsold the pessimists by 20 percent in their first year,
and 57 percent in the second.

So take that, all you sulkers and naysayers. Of course, that study
doesn't mean you have to sell insurance for the rest of your life. It

simply should make you pause and think about the big picture in all this. Here are a few more points to consider when dealing with the inevitable rejection that's bound to happen sooner or later:

1) **Consider the Groucho Marx effect.** You've heard his famous saying: "I wouldn't want to be a member of any club that would have me as a member." Well, many students follow this axim as if it were law. One wonderful student, Scarlett, really wanted to attend a certain well-known southern school . . . until, that is, she was actually accepted. At that point, just as in chapter 13 we mentioned could happen, all of her energies turned to the one college that had put her on the wait-list. When she was, in fact, accepted from the wait-list, she began having doubts again!

Know that if a college admits you, it might *actually* consider you a good match. There are studies of guppies—yes, the little fish—in which the female guppy is infinitely more interested in the male guppy when he's accompanied by another female. When the male is alone, however, she barely glances at him. Now, we're not suggesting that we as humans are on the level of guppies . . . okay, maybe we are. The point is this: there's clearly something on a deep-down level that urges us to be a part of something "special." If other people want something, by golly, we want it too.

A former student, while at NYU, worked as a club promoter in the city. Simply, he'd help rally people to a club, and, once a crowd had gathered . . . guess what? Other people would want to come in. The same effect is what makes people pay big bucks for airport VIP rooms. There's always another level people want to aspire to so they feel that they're special, among the select few. Bah humbug. We're all special. If Dr. Seuss didn't convince you of that, no one can. As Mark Twain said, "In order to make a man or a boy covet a thing, it is only necessary to make the thing difficult to obtain."

2) **Remember the "it's not you, it's me" thing?** As the director of a hotshot local college told us, "Almost all the kids who apply can do the work. We know this, but we're trying to create a class composed of individuals with complementary attributes."

3) **Be Buddhist and remove your ego from the equation.** (Sit cross-legged and repeat: ohm . . .)

4) **Keep in mind that while everyone else in your senior class SEEMS to be receiving great news, it's not true.** People, after all, tend to only talk about their successes. Similarly, in the dating world, almost everyone else seems to be in a happy, perfect relationship. It's vital to know that many people are going through what you're going through—even if you might not see it on the surface.

5) **Give yourself two weeks to work through the hurt.** Then move on.

---

### Handling Rejection

1) Get out of the house NOW.

2) Run five miles.

3) Go to an action movie.

4) Treat yourself to a giant chocolate sundae with extra whipped cream (but *after* the five-mile run).

5) Know that you weren't meant to be with that person because, quite simply, you're not with that person. Be with someone who sees what you've got to offer.

6) Fill your room with flowers—unless, that is, you're allergic.

7) Call a fun friend.

8) Know that you'll likely go through stages, with denial, bargaining, loneliness, anger, and blame being among them. The last stage, of course, is acceptance.

9) Avoid romantic comedies.

10) Convince yourself that you were planning on breaking up with that person anyway. Denial can come in handy.

## Chapter 15

# Taking a Break or "Finding Yourself"

## The gap year

*"To die and not be lost, is the real blessing of a long life."*
—Lao-Tzu

An option that's continuingly growing in popularity is the "gap" year, a time when high school students take a semester or a year off before college. This can be a great idea if you're feeling burned out from high school or just want some time to think about things before getting back on the academic treadmill. Lynda still regrets not taking a break before her freshman year. If you're thinking about a year off, however, you need to keep a few things in mind.

First, you should still apply to all the colleges as you normally would during senior year. Then, upon acceptance, you can talk to the school you choose about holding off a year or even just a semester. "Aww, shucks," you might be saying, "one of the whole points of taking a year off is to avoid doing applications during senior year." Wrong. Every now and then a student will opt to do the entire application process the year after he's graduated, and he always regrets it. It's amazing, but once you're out of high school and have lost your momentum, it's really tough to get back into doing what you need to do to get things together. When you were a senior, what would have been a simple walk down the hall to the registrar's office or a chat with a teacher about a recommendation letter, turns into multiple phone calls and voice mails, appointments, and trips back to high school.

Second, make sure you have a definite plan for when you're gone. Though you don't have to build a particle accelerator, you do need to do something productive. We've seen students who leave and think they'll work part-time at a coffee shop and just sort of "find themselves." Unfortunately, they usually end up "finding themselves" on a couch at home, wishing they'd gone to college. Having a specific plan also impresses the college you've chosen and almost always guarantees a "yes" to a request for a deferral. We've had students take the year off to work in a local theater, others who go abroad, and others who do service projects. A particularly adventuresome student drove around the country in his beat-up SUV in search of the best rock climbing. Another divided up her year into three parts: a travel component in Spain, a service piece, and then, at last, work as a white-water guide in Colorado. If you're not prepared to strike out on your own, there are various organizations, books, and websites to give you a hand. Just to begin, you might check out: www.gapyear.com, www.takingtimeoff. com, www.studyabroad.com, and Princeton Review's book, *Taking Time Off*.

Third, realize that the reality of a gap year involves some challenges you might not be aware of. Seeing your peers go off to college and come back with stories of new friends and excitement is tough—if, that is, you're not doing something interesting yourself.

But this *can* be a great time for you to learn more about the big world out there *and* about who you are!

## Chapter 16

# Love the One You're With

### Making your choice and liking it

*"I love her too, but our neuroses just don't match."*
—ARTHUR MILLER

So maybe you got into your "dream" school, maybe not. Either way, know that there will still be issues—dreamy as the college might be. Remember earlier when we told you about Lynda's advisee who went to his dream school and then wanted to transfer because it couldn't possibly live up to all the fantasies he'd created about it? He's not alone.

Another student, Tristan, who had also gone off to his dream school, returned to chat with Eric after his freshman year. He reported that he hadn't been all that happy at first, but that he was learning to like it there. Wise counselor Eric theorized that Tristan had expected too much. He said, "You had built college up to be this life-altering, over-the-top cool experience, in which all the professors are brilliant and empathetic, the girls all look like Penélope Cruz, and the friends are like characters from, well, *Friends*. In the end, you realized that it's still just a school, and you still have homework." Tristan nodded at the description.

How often do we hear people say about the college experience, "These are the best years of your life"? No wonder unrealistic expectations are the norm!

But fortunately, you're in better shape than most aspiring freshmen. You made your list carefully, including only colleges you'd like to attend; you balanced long shots, targets, and good bets; you've resisted any urges to "trophy hunt" for the greatest number of acceptances; and you knew better than to fall in love with just one school.

To put things in perspective, remember that, first and foremost, education is what you make of it. There are chowderheads at Harvard and brilliant minds at the local community college. If you're motivated, you can learn pretty much whatever you want to wherever you are. Of course, a place like Harvard tends to provide the atmosphere and peer group conducive to high-level learning, but if you're disciplined, that's not necessary.

Second, there are fantastic professors everywhere. If you're planning on going to a brand-name school just because of some celebrity professor, chances are you'll never even take a class with the person anyway. And there are small, out-of-the-way places that, for whatever reason, attract a great faculty. Fort Lewis College here in Colorado, for example, is located in beautiful Durango, and the professors we've met—all engaging, lively people—teach there in large part because they love the outdoors and the charming town.

But what happens when more than one college from your carefully made list wants you? Maybe they've even given you merit-based aid (that "please come" money we talked about earlier). Current students are calling you to talk about all the advantages of attending Dreamboat U, and some professors have emailed you. It's as if you have too many suitors, each one trying to sweep you off your feet.

If several schools want you, this doesn't mean that the counselor made you "shoot too low" (as one student recently told her counselor). It simply means you have a good list. Another sign that you have a good list is that you honestly can't decide between one of your good bets and one of your long shots. A former student from Kent Denver found herself accepted to both Dartmouth, a long shot, and Knox, a good bet. Which did she end up choosing? Interestingly, it was Knox.

Now, to be fair, we have to add that Knox did offer her more money, but that wasn't the entire reason for her choice. She was enticed by the strong programs in both computer science and creative writing available at Knox.

One of Lynda's advisees, Venus, who was already an accomplished film-maker, recently found herself in a pleasant dilemma. She was 95% certain that film would be her life's work, and so she felt that Emerson's focused program was an excellent option. She also knew that she loved Boston. To give herself another possibility in that great college city, Venus applied to Boston University, a larger school with more varied programs. When both accepted her, she felt torn. Would it be a mistake to focus too narrowly too early? What about social life? Further complicating things, her parents, who secretly leaned toward her attending BU, refused to weigh in. In late April, Venus came to Lynda's office for help. Now, through the years, Lynda has steadfastly refused to choose a college for her students, believing that this big decision is part of growing up. Making no exception for Venus, Lynda took out a legal pad, wrote the names of both colleges on it, and made columns for advantages and disadvantages of attending each one. Then she asked Venus to tell her what to write. As Venus talked, she listened to her own voice. After half an hour, without looking at Lynda's notes, she realized that she had come to her own conclusions. She was sure about wanting a career in film, and she was sure about attending Emerson.

Another of Lynda's advisees, Cupid, an aspiring politician, had early in life somehow fallen in love with the idea of attending Georgetown. Was he a well-qualified candidate? Yes! Cupid was a super-student, outspoken editor of the newspaper, incredibly talented star of every play and musical, and even student body president in his senior year. To frost the cupcake (if you're into that sort of thing), he played more-than-respectable tennis and was a dedicated volunteer in the Republican Party. But remember what we said about admission to schools like Georgetown? Hard to predict! You guessed it. He didn't get in. Amherst won this guy for some pretty intriguing reasons. One of them was that he'd decided he wanted to be in a different political climate, that he wanted a place that would challenge some of his assumptions. There weren't many Young Republicans in his freshman class, and his newspaper columns stirred up controversy. By sophomore year, he was elected to student government; he sang with a great a cappella group;

and he became a tour leader for the admission office, going on to become a green dean (alumnus and staff member) after graduation. He told Lynda that he wondered how he'd ever even thought of attending any other college! After various conversations throughout his college years, Cupid concluded that Georgetown had become some sort of fetish for him—something more than a college, something to strive for and win. Once he realized that wasn't happening, this bright, self-aware guy made a logical choice for logical reasons.

Now, we're guessing you're really worried about all the poor kids who can't decide among all the schools that accepted them. You feel their suffering, don't you? More likely, you want to wring their necks and make them *really* suffer, but know that chances are, you'll also have some choices to make (especially if you actually took our advice in this book!). Believe it or not, the decision really can be stressful—even if it is a stress that's infinitely better than getting in nowhere.

One student of Eric's found herself feeling beaten up in the early stages of the admission process (translated: she got turned down by the first two schools she heard from and waitlisted at her favorite). She quickly readjusted her sights (an important skill for the process) and expressed a sincere interest to her favorite. Three weeks later, she was accepted into all of her good bets and two of her targets and off the wait list for both of her long-shot schools. By the time she'd gotten to the end of the process, she was torn about what to do. The glamour of the long-shot acceptances was as tempting as it was unexpected. Ultimately, she chose the school that had been her favorite all along.

How to choose when the cards are on the table and everyone's waiting for you? Many students end up sounding like angst-addled Goldilocks. "This school is the right size," they'll say, "but this one has a better English program, and then this other one is in the coolest place. Isn't there one that's 'just right'?"

To help with your decision, we have another list, of course (this is, after all, what we do). First and foremost, however, remember that wherever you go, you will be fine if you decide you're committed to the education. Think back to what we talked about back in the beginning of this book. Remember those long-range studies suggesting that it really doesn't matter where you go to school but what you do once there? Or all those presidents attending no-name institutions? Or—just as compelling—all those knuckleheads attending big-name places? Education really and truly is what you make of it, so don't go too crazy during this decision phase. As we've discussed, whether you choose Harvard or Colorado State, college is, after all, still just college. Now, as long as you keep this big picture in mind, here are a few things to consider if you have to decide . . .

## FIVE THINGS YOU CAN DO WHEN YOU JUST CAN'T MAKE A DECISION . . .

1) Find out from your guidance counselor about any alumni from your high school attending the colleges and call them. If there aren't any, call the admission offices and see if there are any other students you could talk to. (During this call, refer to some of those questions from "the visit" chapter.)

2) Visit again, if possible. Some admission offices refer to April, when students are visiting their favorites, as "the victory tour." Consider NOT going during one of the Campus Preview Weekends. Though there'll certainly be fun things happening on these preview weekends, we've had students come back with an absolutely unrealistic sense of a place, decide to go, and then end up disappointed. Also, if visiting, be extra-aware of how irritating the travel is. Maybe the plane and shuttle-bus ride that didn't seem like all that big a deal last summer would start to grow old if done several times a year.

3) Go back online and look up the departments of subjects that interest you. You might find some professor bios and coursework that intrigue you more at one place than another.

4) Think back to how schools treated you. Maybe someone in the admission office made a nice comment about your essay, or perhaps you had a meaningful chat with a professor or a coach while visiting. Sometimes, how you're treated during the process reflects how you'll be treated once there.

5) Read the school newspapers, comparing what's happening on each campus. You'll learn what the big issues are as well as what the social scene is like.

Once you've made your own decision, easy or difficult though it may be, we recommend that you practice what the psychologists call "reduction of cognitive dissonance." These are big words for a simple idea: love the once you're with! Like the song says, *You've got to accentuate the positive, eliminate the negative, latch on to the affirmative, and don't mess with Mr. In-Between* . . .

## Chapter 17

# When Things Go South

## The transfer

*"As it will be the right of all, so it will be the duty of some, definitely to prepare for a separation, amicably if they can, violently if they must."*

—Josiah Quincy

Occasionally it happens, and it's a sad but common aspect of our modern world: the break-up. While a college transfer is nowhere near as sad and traumatic an experience as the end of a serious relationship, it can still feel like a pretty big deal. Though we've seen many students think they want to transfer after the first semester, more often than not, after waiting another semester or so, they end up just fine. Sometimes a transfer has to do with expectations; other times it's finding the right group of friends; and even other times, it's just because of weather. In many situations, the student will like the school but will just want to be closer to home. Or farther from home. When thinking of a transfer, however, you want to be extra careful about keeping your college grades high. Additionally, you want to maintain a positive attitude. When the new college to which you're applying asks why, state the reason as something good the new place offers rather than something negative about the current place. Otherwise, you might just come off as a whiner.

One of Lynda's advisees wanted to transfer to NYU, and he did everything right. He was at the top of his freshman class at his original college, and by investigating a little, he learned that the main reasons students leave NYU is that the place is just too urban for them. Turns out that the guy knew the Big Apple well and was eager for exactly that kind of big-city experience. So he salted his essay with specific references to what he liked about big city life (Van Gogh's *Starry Night*, hot bagels, and being able to hear five different languages in the same subway car). He made it clear that although he was fine where he was, he was looking for something even better and that he wasn't running away from anything.

Are you ready to transfer? Ask yourself the following questions before making any hasty decision:

- Have you grown? (After all, if you haven't, why would another college want to take you as a transfer student?)

- Have you taken tough courses where you are now?

- Have you given this whole notion of transferring enough time?

- What is really inspiring this change in the first place? Is it something fickle like a roommate, or is it something more substantive like the intellectual climate of a campus?

One of Eric's former students, a bright, down-to-earth young woman, chose an academically high-caliber university in the south. Though many of Eric's former students had attended this university and loved it, this particular girl loathed every second there. The female students were much too into the whole "Southern Belle" thing for this young woman, who was more interested in social justice and books than what she'd be wearing to the next debutante ball. She left after one semester to attend a large state university back home, where she found her niche and a happier social life.

### How to Deal with a Break-Up

1) Don't hold a grudge; forgive and try to forget.

2) Don't recount all the negative experiences that led you to separate.

3) Look forward, not back.

4) Find someone to rebound with. (Okay, maybe not . . .)

# Chapter 18

# Marriage

## How to succeed in college: tips from former students

> *"My definition of marriage . . . it resembles a pair of shears,*
> *so joined that they cannot be separated; often moving in opposite*
> *directions, yet always punishing anyone*
> *who comes between them."*
>
> —SYDNEY SMITH

So you're in college. Now what? Your teary-eyed parents have just left—finally—and you're in your room with a roommate you've just met, who's now putting up posters you're not sure you want to live with all year. You don't know if you should go to the freshman meet-and-greet, or if it'll be too corny. You sit down on your bed and wonder what lies ahead.

Since it's been a few years since we've been in college, we've collected words of wisdom from former students about what they think is important. Some of these items are big, others small, but they're all meant to help you see what it's like.

Here's what they offer . . .

"Location of the school might seem superficial, but area/weather/and ease with which students can get to a city really are important factors. For example, I know people who thought they could handle cloudiness but just can't."

"Don't go to school while you have a serious boyfriend/girlfriend far away. The only people I know that are homesick or miserable here left a boyfriend/girlfriend at home or at another school. Seriously, it sounds harsh, but it really hinders your friend-making abilities when you're always missing someone."

"If you're not sure what you want to study, you might want a bigger university instead of a liberal arts college. No one ever told me that, but at a lot of the schools I looked at, there weren't great communications or sociology programs, which I've become interested in now."

—*Madeline, University of Southern California*

"Be patient when you get to college. Because everyone is living in the same area, college life tends to move very quickly, and you can easily feel as though you are behind. It may take a few months for your life to fall into place, but if you are patient and willing to try new things (take classes in new disciplines, join an extracurricular activity) you will find your niche. And once you find your group, remember to slow down every once in a while!"

—*Elena, Harvard*

"You'll meet more people if you don't live with a close friend from high school, but sometimes it's just great to be with people you know well and trust. So, I'd say that if you do decide to room with a good buddy, be aware that you'll have to make more of an effort to meet new people."

"Join clubs early. Time management goes better when you have a lot to do."

—*Steven, NYU*

"If you're an only child, remember to remain flexible. You'll have some adjusting to do when you have to share your living space."

"Go somewhere you can shine."

—*Anne, UVA*

"College classes are different from high school. There are only a few grades, so you need to keep up with your reading and attend class, even though nobody is taking attendance!"

"Take classes outside your major."

"Get to know your professors—it'll help you do well in school!"

"Go abroad."

—*Natalie, Colorado University*

"The best thing that could prepare a person for college, more than just a few lines of advice, is a simple understanding of how college functions. I don't think I ever really comprehended that being prepared for college mostly entailed structure: in my work, in my room, in my socializing, and in my whole life. I find that what I really pursue now that I am at Stanford is efficiency. I feel that I need to finish a huge pile of work as quickly as possible so that I can make time for other things. I feel that I need to compartmentalize my life. While this might sound like a drag, it's definitely worth the effort. Wherever this craving for efficiency comes from (maybe a worry that college will be over before I get a chance to do everything I want to?), I wish that I'd recognized this necessity the first day I arrived on campus."

—*Joe, Stanford*

"Don't be afraid to use all the resources available to you—such as tutors, for example. Kids who were at the top of their class in high school might feel bashful about getting help in college, and they shouldn't."

—*Brianna, Washington University*

"Make sure you get to know your professors. Go see them during their office hours at the beginning of each semester. Introduce yourself, and ask questions like 'How long should I study for the next test?' so that you can understand their expectations. Once I started putting in the amount of time they suggested, it made all the difference."

"Figure out the sorts of tests you do well on, and choose classes that play to your strengths. For example, I don't do well with multiple choice, so I shop for courses where the tests are mostly essay. I'm really in my element when I can take a class that has no tests, and the grades are based entirely on papers. "

"One more thing: Work hard and also play hard!"

*—Chris, Davidson*

"One of the most important things I wish I had not done was bring so much stuff with me to college. I had to figure out what to do with all of it during exam week when I also needed to be studying, and since I was moving out of the dorms, in-dorm storage was not available to me. I would definitely advise everyone to limit what they bring."

"High school only matters insofar as it has made you the person you are when you enter college. Nobody cares whether you went to Exeter or a public school with poor funding, but what does matter is who you are and what you do once you get to the university. Some of the most limited individuals I know here at U. Chicago are the people I hear talking most often about the glories and woes of their high school days. It is as though they have forgotten that they are alive in the present moment, or perhaps they are afraid to face the present moment and would rather hide in and be defined by their pasts."

*—Megan, University of Chicago*

"I wish that I had understood better that college is not the ultimate answer to living a happy and fulfilling life. I know that sounds obvious, but all through high school, there is so much emphasis on getting into a good college, that on some level, I think I thought, 'Well, I did that right. Everything else should fall into place.' And it doesn't. College is just one step. It's lots of fun. You learn, you grow up some, you graduate. And then the real world kicks you around. I found that very shocking."

"I think if I had understood better how competitive and indifferent the real world ACTUALLY IS, I might have spent a little more time appreciating the network that college can offer. I might have thought more about how to position myself to ease my entry into the real world."

"Yale seems to think it's good to shelter its students. You get the pure Yale experience that way. But as a result, all the Yale grads I know had a very rocky first year out of college. I imagine that's true about graduates at many of the top schools. Those universities tell you over and over how competent you are (and you ARE competent), but they forget to tell you that the real world is NOT a meritocracy. The real world works by referrals, networks, and assertive self-promotion. Your actual abilities only matter once you're already hired. So college is just as important for the network it provides as for the actual skills and knowledge it imparts. This is kind of a downer message to give to freshmen, so I think that's why no one ever says it."

*—Erika, Yale*

"As most of my friends are finishing their sophomore year, their reflections on the long road of college life behind them have in turn fascinated, upset, and comforted me. I have always heard detailed and honest accounts of some of my friends' experiences over the past two years, but only recently have some of my other friends divulged their honest feelings about college. I hear about a whole spectrum of emotions, depression marking one end and elation marking the other, with feelings like loneliness, fear, confidence, and satisfaction in the middle. I think that feeling emotions on the bottom half of the spectrum in college is the big elephant in the middle of the room that nobody talks about. I feel as if far too many people are eager to share their amazing college stories and much too afraid to vocalize the difficulties they have encountered."

"At the beginning of freshman year, for example, my friends and acquaintances at other schools and at Williams, as well, were terribly eager to tell me about their many, many friends and how much fun they were having. I, and as I now know, many others, had made friends, but certainly we hadn't found these intimate and exciting friendships that everyone else seemed to be enjoying. At a moment where we were already feeling lonely, their stories made us feel so much more isolated—as if we were failing."

"If everyone weren't so afraid to admit to having a hard time and facing challenges, a very beneficial sense of solidarity would emerge. People could face their challenges together. So my advice to incoming freshmen would be that everyone in college, especially at some point in their first two years, struggles with feelings of isolation. The glowing reports of college are often embellished for fear of sounding inadequate. And if these glowing reports and stories are true, then they often occur only after the student has overcome a few obstacles. The challenges students encounter range anywhere from a lack of self-esteem, to not finding compatible friends immediately, to accidentally befriending mean people, and even to suffering from depression. Overcoming these challenges makes the happiness one finds all the more rewarding and renders these glowing reports of college wholly truthful and warranted. If you aren't happy, know that you are not alone. Once you patiently wade through the swamp of difficult times, the happiness you will encounter is so very sweet."

"If all this is too long and wordy, the other piece of advice I have is short. Say, 'Hi!' to or smile at everyone you pass on campus. I think that far too many people walk with their heads down. The power of a simple smile between strangers can be really great. Two of my strongest friendships at school started by exchanging smiles that slowly developed into hello's and then into conversations and now friendships!"

"One last thing: Even if you went to a serious, college-prep high school, realize that you'll face academic pressures in college that you weren't expecting. Yes, there's stress in high school, but it's a softer form of stress."

*—Lauren, Williams*

"Match the location of the school according to your personality. For example, think whether you'd enjoy having a whole city available to you or if you'd prefer a more rural college where campus life focuses on frat parties."

"No matter how difficult your roommate is, make him think you like him while you're plotting your escape. Most housing forms have stupid questions, but write your sleeping hours, and try to make sure someone pays attention."

"It's good to have a friend from home at your college. That person won't keep you from meeting new people and having your own experiences, and there are lots of times when she/he can be a real comfort as you navigate a new world."

*—Alex, Fordham*

"Coming from a small, private high school, I was used to having close contact with my teachers and really becoming friends with them. I was surprised that this was not the norm at Dartmouth. My advice would be to be assertive in getting to know your professors—you'll have to go to them, because they won't be coming to you in the same way they did in high school. You'll want to form these relationships, but you'll have to make it happen."

*—Lauren, Dartmouth*

"Go to college with a mind open to all sorts of things. You should have some goals connected with what you'd like to accomplish, but be flexible. Also, be ready to make friends with people you might not immediately identify as 'your type.'"

—*Blaine, George Washington*

"I found that college was a balance of activities, school-work, and socializing, and if I were starting over again, I would like to have participated in more of the activist groups on campus. It is incredibly hard to be involved in even one or two worthwhile activities while still getting what you want from classes and having time for friends, but I eventually figured out how to do it. It's tricky to advise people about this, though, since it's very easy to become so over-programmed that you end up doing everything poorly. Finding the right balance is the ticket!"

—*Ben, Stanford*

"The larger the class, the easier it is to fall behind. If you need assistance, be vocal. Speak to your professor and your T.A.—get to know them! Even ask a friend to help you. You don't want your GPA to be ruined by your lack of effort in one class. In college there is much less personal attention. It's your responsibility to stay on top of the work, manage your time, and find help when you need it."

"Even if you have declared your major, I think it's a good idea to broaden your horizons by taking classes in other disciplines. This will expose you to a variety of subjects and give you a chance to meet new people. It's all part of growing as an individual, an essential part of the college experience."

"Go abroad! My most rewarding experience in college was my junior year abroad. During the fall semester, I went to Italy. Georgetown had an exceptional program where a small number of students lived and studied in a beautiful villa outside of Florence. We had an eclectic group of Italian, British, and Dutch professors who taught us Italian language, Renaissance history, art, and literature. Second semester was vastly different but just as memorable. I went to Chile and attended the large public university where I studied with a real variety of individuals from Chile and other countries. My classes with only Chilean students were challenging and exciting, and traveling throughout Chile, Argentina, and Peru opened my eyes. If you don't speak another language, investigate programs that don't require that skill. This is the moment to grow by meeting new people, embarking on adventures, experiencing different ways of living, and learning about other cultures."

—*Noelle, Georgetown*

### Staying in Love, or Keeping the Flame Alive:

1) Never throw your true love's ratty clothes away.

2) Say "yes," almost always.

3) Learn to cook what he or she likes to eat.

4) Pretend you like it when the other person reads boring stuff aloud to you.

5) Love the people your beloved loves.

6) Laugh at his jokes—always.

# Our Random List
# of 76 Colleges We Like

The following is a completely arbitrary list, in no particular order at all, of some schools we think deserve a second glance. There is nothing even remotely scientific or quantifiable about this line-up, and we're fully aware that there are dozens of unbelievably amazing colleges we're not including. These are a few we've had good experiences with but, for whatever reason, aren't quite as "popular" as we think they should be. Either we've visited and liked the place, or former students have attended and spoken highly of it.

The descriptions you'll read are pretty much versions of what we'd say to our students when they ask us for our opinions (minus the "ums" and other filler words, of course). The sound-bite paragraphs are too short to even pretend to be complete, but they'll give you at least a little sense of each place, we hope.

1. **Haverford:** You gotta love the Quakers. If you don't know anything about them other than the oatmeal man, educationally-speaking, you'll find they're worth checking out. Historically Quaker schools (such as Earlham, Guilford, Whittier, and Swarthmore) don't allow fraternities or sororities because of the negative hierarchies they promote. You'll call professors by their first name—because, hey, we're all spiritual equals. And the Society of Friends—the real name of the Quaker church—believes in preaching through actions rather than words. As a result, Quaker schools tend to be hotbeds of activism, global awareness, and community service. On top of all this, Haverford offers a rock-star education and is a place with oodles of smart kids.

2. **William and Mary:** Though Virginia public schools tend not to be all that nice to out-of-staters, William and Mary could go head to head with any Ivy League institution, any day. Located in beautiful and historic Williamsburg, Virginia (a place your parents will love to visit), William and Mary is known for its intellectual rigor and intensity. Pressure-cooker though it might be, the fact that Jon Stewart went there means it's got to have some fun going on, right?

3. **Davidson:** Like the first two, this isn't an easy one to get into either, but we include it because it doesn't get the respect it deserves outside North Carolina. Sure, it almost beat Kansas in the 2008 March Madness, but Davidson is so much more than a David vs. Goliath story in sports. Kids who are high-powered brainiacs in their high schools but like the politeness of the South and get a kick out of sports would enjoy Davidson. All of Eric and Lynda's students who have attended say they've been challenged to no end, but they also loved it. Obsessed with Duke? Think Davidson; academically, it's just as respected, but you'll get more face time with your professors.

4. **Swarthmore:** Swarthmore is known to be a place where true scholars congregate. Remember that story from earlier in the book about the *Sports Illustrated* writer in the locker room of the Swarthmore football team—where the players were discussing Aristotelian philosophy after their loss? That pretty much sums up the place. It's frighteningly tough to get into but worth pursuing if you're a high achiever who doesn't need Yale or Harvard.

5. **Miami U. (Ohio):** NOT to be confused with University of Miami. Students at Miami U. wear shirts saying, correctly, "Miami was a University before Florida was a state." Miami is often ranked as one of the best teaching universities around. Though it has a big-school feel—with big-school parties (since, after all, many fraternities have their founding chapters there)—the school's philosophy promotes plenty of professor-student interaction. Eric taught some beginning Spanish sections for a while there, and even though he had everyone from linebackers to hockey players in those classes, every student was articulate, hardworking, and polite.

6. **U. of Montana:** This school is great not only for outdoorsy kids but also for students who want a public school where they won't feel overwhelmed. Solid academics, including an outstanding English department, and a beautiful college town make this a place to check out.

7. **U. of Wyoming:** Similar to the University of Montana in that it's one of those not-too-big state schools, Wyoming has the added advantage of having lots of money from the oil business. Beyond having all sorts of connections to the oil and gas industry, though, the University of Wyoming is also heavily involved in alternative energies. Go Cowboys!

8. **Whitman:** Don't let the town's odd name fool you. Out in the middle of the Pacific Northwest's wine country—as well as fields of the region's famous sweet onions—Walla Walla, which means "land of many waters," is a picturesque community that's proud of its college and rightfully so. Whitman is a place where soft-spoken intellectuals who enjoy the outdoors would be happy. Eric took a tour there a few years ago, and while walking around on a Sunday night, he met students in dorm rooms, in the theater, and in science labs—all of whom were working away and all of whom seemed genuinely passionate and enthusiastic about what they were studying, acting, or researching. Also, Whitman brings in heavy-hitter speakers and organizes cool cultural events, so you won't feel isolated.

9. **Colorado College:** This liberal arts college in the otherwise con-servative Colorado Springs—just a few miles from the Air Force Academy—is an absolute gem. It's no longer "undiscovered" on the national level, but it still doesn't have the name recognition it should. Its block program is what the school is perhaps most fa-mous for, and though the block has its critics, our students who've attended love how taking one course at a time allows them to explore a topic in depth. The academic work is tough, but the student body tends to be pretty laid-back and just as focused on outdoor activities as they are on hitting the books. CC is cur-rently ranked as one of the best values among national liberal arts colleges, and it has recently been noted as a small college with one of the highest percentages of grads who go on to join the Peace Corps.

10. **Guilford:** Here's another Quaker place, but in North Carolina—which makes it an unusual bastion of liberalism in a southern state. Eric actually attended Guilford, and once he'd visited, it was the only school he decided to apply to. The service work, the study abroad programs, and the authentically friendly students and professors won him over from the first moment. Guilford is great for the protest-loving, earthy student who likes places like Oberlin and Haverford but might not have the SAT scores for them.

11. **Earlham:** Similar to Guilford, but in Richmond, Indiana. Maybe a smidgen more rigorous academically, but similar sorts of global-thinking, curious students.

12. **Dickinson:** This Pennsylvania-based college was able to boast of going global before the term was even trendy. Over half of the classes have an international component, over half the students go abroad, and many of the business courses maintain an international focus. Dickinson also has an organic farm where any student who wants to can volunteer. How cool is that?

13. **Kalamazoo College:** "K," as it's lovingly known by its students, is a hands-on sort of place great for the student who wants to ride the fast track to a career. The school offers a strong liberal arts education, and it encourages students to apply that kind of thinking from the moment they arrive. The "K" plan arranges career development and internship opportunities for students, beginning the summer after their freshman year, often finding places with Kalamazoo alumni for them. During sophomore or junior year, around 80% of the student body studies abroad, and as seniors, all students must complete a "Senior Individualized Project." Science and pre-med are strong at "K," and the school is ranked high in preparing its grads for work in those fields.

14. **Tulane:** New Orleans, and by association, Tulane, might have a reputation for partying. These days, that reputation doesn't quite match up to the truth. Perhaps as a result of Hurricane Katrina, Tulane has become more focused on community—both its own and the New Orleans community at large—and, while it has pared some departments down, the university has by no means

diminished in quality. Beyond the traditional liberal arts, Tulane offers advanced degrees in everything from architecture to tropical medicine. The student body is diverse, and they're focused on their studies and eager to be involved.

15. **Agnes Scott:** This all-women's college is located about an hour outside of Atlanta on a lovely, tree-filled campus. The school population is tiny, but it boasts a 30+% minority population, and it offers more than 300 internship connections for its students. Speaking and writing receive major academic focus, and the school prides itself on its theme houses.

16. **Emory:** With a $4 billion dollar endowment (much of which comes from Woodruff, the founder of Coca Cola), Emory is doing just fine for itself. Though it has no football team, it has many of the other trappings of a big campus without actually being *big*. The student body looks diverse when you're walking around, and the campus itself, with its red-tiled roofs, looks sort of like an Atlanta version of Stanford. Emory is one of those schools that fits the "not too big, not too small" size category many students want. Also, it provides the research opportunities of a bigger university while not forgetting the face time with professors.

17. **Spelman College:** Spelman is an all-black women's college located in downtown Atlanta, next to its brother school Morehouse and also Clark. The three institutions share a library, and Spelman students can take classes at both of the other schools. Spelman has a consortium with a number of universities across the country—from Dartmouth to Stanford—and many students take advantage of these opportunities. Students speak with pride about personal interactions with their professors, and after a visit, most admitted applicants decide they want to attend.

18. **Beloit:** This Wisconsin college is one of the few small liberal arts colleges in the country with an archaeology program—and a strong one at that! Though students might not make a big deal about their standardized test scores, they're known to be a hardworking and intellectually free-spirited bunch. Beloit thinks of itself as a "three-legged" school, with internships, overseas study, and interdisciplinary connections forming a big part of the cam-

pus identity. Fun tidbits: Beloit hosts a well-attended International Film Festival in January each year, referred to as an alternative to Sundance by *The New York Times*!

19. **University of Wisconsin (Madison):** The University of Wisconsin is a big state school with a respected academic reputation. The town of Madison always ranks as one of the best towns to live in, and students love it there. If you're a student who's worried about getting lost in the crowd, Wisconsin isn't for you, but if you're a motivated sort, it's worth checking out.

20. **Berea:** This wonderful little school in Kentucky would be a gem even if it weren't FREE. You read correctly. Since its inception at the end of the nineteenth century, Berea has provided full tuition scholarships for all who attend. A labor grant is part of this scholarship, which means that every student works on campus as part of his or her package. Also, though the school was designed to serve students from Appalachia, it reserves a sizeable chunk of its admission slots for applicants from throughout the world.

21. **University of Denver:** DU used to be more of a regional school, but as its endowment has grown, so, too, has its presence as a national player. The Daniels College of Business is well-respected, and the Hotel/Tourism/Restaurant-Management program gives its grads a great foundation for the future. DU is located in a low-keyed area of the city with easy walking access to coffee shops and restaurants, and the light rail that runs right through campus takes students downtown for free. As an interesting tidbit, Condoleeza Rice studied there under Madeline Albright's father. Also, while many universities talk about looking at the "whole" student, DU is a school that really does. The multi-layered interview forms a huge part of a candidate's application, as do the essays and teacher recs.

22. **University of Colorado (Boulder):** Beyond the fact that Boulder is a picturesque town filled with great restaurants and wealthy bohemians (maybe a good thing, maybe not), it also backs right up to the Flatirons—the mountains that jut up from the plains in Boulder's backyard. Even if Boulder weren't so cool, CU would still be a great school to consider in its own right. With several Nobel laureates in the science departments, CU offers cutting-

edge research opportunities in everything from aerospace engineering to alternative energies. Lynda got her MA and teaching certification there, and she also taught first-year Spanish.

23. **Colorado State University:** Fort Collins, the town where CSU is located, is more of a "real people" Boulder, but the town center—which is where the University is located—offers plenty of non-chain restaurants, bars, and ice cream shops. Like CU, CSU is also known for its science programs, but it earns national recognition for its department of veterinary science.

24. **Salve Regina:** You drive out to Newport, across the sweeping expanse of bridge. You drive past the church where JFK and Jackie married, past Eisenhower's summer home, and you turn the corner and see, fronting the vast Atlantic Ocean, the *really* big estates—those built by the Vanderbilts and Astors, just to name-drop two. In this setting, with the rocky, English-looking coast to the right, you pull up to a castle that makes you feel like you're a character in a Jane Austen novel. Or, as another counselor told Eric in hushed tones, "It's a Harry Potter movie." Salve Regina is a Catholic school, but, since it was founded by the Sisters of Mercy, tolerance and social justice are key values.

25. **University of Rhode Island:** This is one of those state schools that doesn't overwhelm. The campus is picture-perfect with its Gothic architecture, and URI is a great place for students interested in either pharmacology or oceanography. Though, as with any state school, it offers virtually every other major imaginable, these two programs are nationally recognized. Robert Ballard, the guy who located the sunken Titanic? He's a professor here.

26. **Bryant:** If you like business but aren't quite sure if your grades match up to a Babson or Bentley, this could be a fantastic school for you. The campus looks a little like a corporate park, but don't let the lack of Georgian architecture fool you. The university has articulated a well-thought-out vision for getting its grads ready for the real world. While some schools talk about helping their charges get more access to technology as well as become more globally-minded, Bryant actually does more than just talk. Every

student receives a state-of-the-art laptop, and every sophomore is required to go abroad.

27. **University of Chicago:** This is the place for the no-messing-around student who doesn't feel the need to loosen up all that much. It's like one of the Ivies, but slightly easier to get into (or so the statistics indicate because applicants largely self-select) and tougher once you are in. The faculty has received just about every accolade you could imagine, and they're also more accessible than you'd think for a school of almost 12,000. We particularly like the interdisciplinary approach where, for example, poets study physics and engineers study music. Lynda was wowed by the fact that university busses operate at regular intervals, taking students to and from the city center. A tour guide told her that she likes to do her calculus homework at the Art Institute!

28. **UBC:** No, this isn't the "University of Boston College" (which wouldn't make sense anyway), but, rather, the University of British Columbia. One of our former students is there and loves it. UBC sports the wide range of course offerings that the big universities do in the States, and it's located in one of the coolest cities in the world, Vancouver, a place where you can take a city bus to the mountains in the morning, kayak in the bay in the afternoon, and go out for sushi at night. (But we almost forgot—you'd be studying anyway, so none of this matters, right?) Our former student is in theater, and since Hollywood does a lot of filming up there, she has found it easier to get acting bits than, say, in Los Angeles. Also, she loves being a representative of one of the more than 100 "foreign" countries there.

29. **Lawrence University:** This is a small college with a bigger college feel—perhaps as a result of the fun town of Appleton where Lawrence is located. Though the university is known for its conservatory, it also offers a full liberal arts buffet that would satisfy anyone. Students consider it challenging but not competitive. As a bonus, the school owns a lodge on the coast of Lake Michigan where 75% of the student body spends at least one weekend each year.

30. **Creighton University:** Don't roll your eyes just because this is a Midwestern school (in Omaha, Nebraska, specifically). Omaha is clean and nice, and you'd be surprised by some of the world-class opportunities available at the University itself. Beyond the fact that its medical program is famous everywhere, Creighton offers every sort of business internship imaginable. And why? Warren Buffet is just one of the local business owners.

31. **Hampshire:** This bucolic college located a stone's throw from Amherst was founded in 1970 as an experiment by U. Mass, Smith, Mount Holyoke, and Amherst to see if students could really take control of their own education. Apparently, at Hampshire, they can. With alums ranging from Ken Burns to Jon Krakauer, the university has evidence that creativity is a prized commodity. Hampshire graduates a large number of future doctors, but it also sends a slew of budding entrepreneurs into the world, too. If independent self-starting isn't your thing, Hampshire isn't for you, but if you like the thought of kicking off your own projects, it's worth checking out. Freshmen begin with what's known as Division I, an academic program that provides some general structure and overview. As sophomores, they move up to Division II, at which point they begin to focus. By senior year, they're working on their own independent projects. Also worthy of note is the fact that Hampshire doesn't do grades—until, of course, a student takes a class at one of the sister colleges.

32. **Clark:** Though Worcester, MA, might not be the most eye-catching city at first blush, Clark shares it with fourteen other colleges—to say nothing of the fact that Boston is a quick train ride away. Being the only site in North America where Sigmund Freud lectured has given Clark's psychology department a big-name reputation. An interesting tidbit is that Clark also boasts an excellent geography program—even on the graduate level.

33. **The College of Wooster:** As *The Fiske Guide to Colleges* says, "Getting admitted is not difficult, but graduating takes work." National fraternities were banned in the '40's because of the perceived snob factor, and all students set up independent projects they work on during their last year.

34. **Oberlin:** Oberlin is famous for being the first coed college in the country, and it's also known for having a phenomenal music conservatory. Beyond this, however, Oberlin is an all-around fantastic liberal arts college. The students are known to be highly intellectual and engaged but more community-oriented (and service-centered) than competitive. Several of our really interesting, individualistic grads have gone there and loved it.

35. **Knox:** Knox is situated in Galesburg, Illinois. If it were near Boston or San Francisco, its application numbers would zoom through the roof. Simply, Knox is a great little school with flexible academic structures, a strong creative writing program, and a surprisingly varied population of international students. As an interesting historical aside, Knox was the site of one of the famous Lincoln-Douglas debates (and Lincoln climbed through a window as he took the stage). Also worthy of mention is the fact that Knox has a magical ability to bring in some of the most in-demand speakers for its graduation. Bill Clinton spoke in 2007, Stephen Colbert in 2006, and Barack Obama in 2005.

36. **Alleghany College:** You have to enjoy small-town living to be okay with Alleghany College, but this cozy campus hidden away in the Alleghany Mountains is a gem. Students who want a well-rounded liberal arts experience and who want to be reasonably challenged but not crushed would like it here.

37. **St. Louis University:** SLU is a Jesuit university whose latest president insisted on transforming the campus into a "garden in the city." The students are friendly, and they're way more diverse than you'd ever guess. Aeronautical engineering, criminal justice/forensic science, and theology are just three of the popular majors. The Jesuit mission encourages students to strive for a more just and humane world.

38. **Carnegie Mellon University:** Like bagpipes? CMU offers a major, amazingly. Beyond this fun factoid, Carnegie Mellon is known for its fascinating mix of engineers, computer science types, and drama/theater students. A gaggle of big-name actors graduated from Carnegie Mellon, and you might have heard about some of the exploits of the engineers through their robotics competitions. CMU has a highly-ranked play-writing program. Its departments

of cognitive psychology, musical theater, and creative writing are also big draws; and two economics professors are Nobel laureates. If you like history, the University houses a rare books/documents collection that, along with one of the four *original* copies of the Bill of Rights, also contains documents from Newton, Shakespeare, Charles Dickens, and Copernicus—just for starters.

39. **Ohio Wesleyan:** Though located in small-town Ohio, Ohio Wesleyan manages to attract a student body comprised of almost a quarter "multi-cultural" students. Business and science are both strong (with zoology being a biggie), and the college prides itself on its tight-knit community—as well as professors who notice when you're not in class.

40. **Scripps:** Scripps's campus looks like a cross between a beautiful Spanish convent and a spa. But don't let the fact that it's an all-female institution scare you away (unless, of course, you're a boy). Studying in the middle of the Claremont consortium, you'd literally be taking classes at your choice of other great colleges. "It's like having the best of both worlds," a tour guide told Eric when he took a tour a few summers ago. Students tend to be globally involved, intellectually vibrant individuals. Lynda notes that the dorms seem more like stately homes than college housing, and she smiled when a guy from Pitzer once swore that the food in Scripps's dining room (from the same food service as Pitzer's) tasted better.

41. **Fort Lewis College:** Located in the stunningly beautiful mountain town of Durango, Fort Lewis is a great place for the kid who maybe didn't hit his or her potential in high school. The professors tend to be there because they want to be, and as a result, also tend to be dedicated educators. Fort Lewis, because of a federal grant from years ago, boasts a sizeable Native American population on campus.

42. **Whittier:** Though at first glance, Whittier might not seem to have the most glamorous campus, chalk that up to the anti-materialism of its Quaker founders. Even so, Lynda was impressed recently by the beautiful new library and technology center. Located in Los Angeles, Whittier is a school that cares about the values of its

students and offers a wide range of inter-disciplinary, "paired" courses for the intellectually curious. For high achievers, there's the Scholars Program where juniors and seniors can do independent projects. You might find a few regional kids there who don't quite "get" the Quaker thing, but you'll also find a number of students deeply engaged in the problems of the world. Fun side note: The president's house was used in the filming of the first, pre-Antonio Banderas, *Zorro*.

43. **Warren Wilson College:** Located in the beautiful mountains of Asheville, North Carolina, Warren Wilson is a hotspot for liberal intellectuals in the South. Students contribute 150 hours of volunteer service, and they work paying jobs, too. Popular majors include environmental studies, outdoor leadership, creative writing, and some of the usual suspects, such as art, biology and English.

44. **Sewanee:** Okay, not to focus too much on a campus's aesthetic appeal, but Sewanee has to have one of the prettiest campuses around. Some might refer to it as "Mayberry on a mountain," and with the college president being mayor of the town, that description might not be too far off! Its location on a mountain top in Tennessee causes students to slap the roofs of their cars when entering and leaving college property. And why? To pick up their guardian angels, of course. Professors tend to wear their black academic gowns when they teach, and members of some of Sewanee's honor societies do, too. The University of the South (as it's also known) is a great place for more conservative students who like nature but who don't mind working as hard as they play.

45. **St. John's (Maryland and Santa Fe):** Because of its huge reputation in academic circles, most people are surprised to hear that the St. John's student body consists of only 450 students. Famous for its "great books" program, St. John's is proud of the fact that it has NO conventional textbooks. Instead, "Johnnies" read from a vast list of original texts, with authors ranging from Descartes to Aristotle to Cervantes. Seminars are designed to give a broad overview of these readings, and then the texts are examined more closely in the tutorials. St. John's provides such an old-school edu-

cation that it ends up being amazingly progressive. One tradition, for example, is known as the Don Rags. After every semester, all of a student's "tutors" (professors) sit at a table. With the student present, they talk about him or her in the third person. While at first this experience might seem a little daunting, it provides students with real tools for self-awareness—to say nothing of amazing preparation for grad school and beyond. Simply, you have to be an intellectual powerhouse to attend, but don't be fooled by St. John's easy-looking acceptance numbers. Applicants tend to limit themselves to a very self-selecting pool. Every St. John's student takes the same classes and reads the same books as every other person in his or her year, and while some might find this claustrophobic, others see it as liberating. St. John's has no fraternities or sororities, and apart from fencing, it has no intercollegiate sports, either. Lynda, a New Mexico native, adds that Santa Fe is about as close to paradise as a person can get while still on earth.

46. **U. of Rochester:** Haven't heard of U. of Rochester? You should. If you like Vanderbilt and Wash. U., then Rochester should be on your list, too. At 4,500 students, it's a great size for most students, and though the cold can be pretty rough in the winter, the campus itself is stunning—while being close to a real city. The university offers grad programs in education, medicine, nursing, dentistry, and music. With money from George Eastman, Bausch and Lomb, and John D. Rockefeller, the University of Rochester is able to take care of itself both aesthetically as well as academically. Lynda, who was treated to a dinner in the Memorial Art Gallery during a counselor tour, found the collection truly impressive. Interestingly, it's one of the few university-affiliated art museums in the country that also serves as a community resource. The sports are D-III, so if you want a decent-sized school with research opportunities but don't need the high-powered sports, Rochester is perfect.

47. **Union College:** One of Eric's former students is currently at Union and loves it. She was a brilliant girl who hadn't quite found her groove in high school—either on the academic or extracurricular levels. Within one semester at Union, she was taking classes towards her MBA, leading the crew team (a sport she had never

tried before), and heading up a social service group on campus. Nearby Schenectady, NY, might not win over many aficionados, but it provides the city basics any student would need.

48. **Skidmore College:** We've met a number of grads from Skidmore. One claimed it was a "theater school," another said it was a "lacrosse college," and another said it was great for international kids. We tend to think it's all of the above. Though historically, Skidmore has been known for its performing arts programs, it's a safe bet to call it an eclectic place. Because it's located in scenic Saratoga Springs, your parents will want to visit, too. (Which isn't as bad a thing as you might think . . .)

49. **Hamilton:** The "college on the hill" offers the quintessential liberal arts experience. Preppiness and grunginess seem pretty well balanced—in part, perhaps, because the campus is divided into a "light" side and a "dark" side. Historically, this comes from the electric grid and the fact that the dark side would stay dark longer after a blackout, but the yin-yang image can also serve as an extended metaphor for campus life. The sides are just stereotypes, but one side is known as the artsy, "crunchy" side, while the other is the more athletic, Greek-oriented, and conservative. Perhaps even more important than any talk of majors or school histories, though, would be the perspective of a Hamilton cafeteria employee. When Eric visited a few years ago, one of the breakfast workers pulled him aside and told him that she "loved Hamilton students." Big praise indeed.

50. **Colgate:** Colgate has something for everyone. It's in upstate New York, has great town-gown relations, offers action-packed athletic competitions (how do you feel about hockey?), and is known for its strong faculty-student relationships. Though it's still fairly Greek-heavy, the school has been making efforts to calm that side of campus life. If you want a place with smart kids who are laid back about how bright they are, Colgate is worth checking out.

51. **Trinity University (San Antonio):** Some of our Colorado students roll their eyes when they hear the word "Texas," but then they visit Trinity U., and they almost always come back singing a different tune. Located in a lovely part of San Antonio, the city

of canals and fantastic salsa verde, Trinity not only offers strong business and engineering, but it also gives its students all they'd want in a good liberal arts program. One of Lynda's students double majored in bio and Spanish, doing pre-med requirements to please his dad and starting a band to please himself. Trinity's sports teams, especially tennis, tend to be real powerhouses. The weather is great and the campus is beautiful, so what's not to like?

52. **Reed:** Located outside Portland, Oregon—a city with both water and mountains nearby—Reed is a perfect place for the high-octane, no-holds-barred intellectual. When Eric visited not long ago, he chatted with students who talked about everything from quantum physics and Shakespeare to Chinese dance and Alaska— and all in a period of about thirty minutes. Reed was founded by a group of East Coast visionaries who wanted to create an intellectual's paradise, away from all the frivolous distractions of supper clubs, fraternities, and football games. Now, some students come to Reed hearing how progressive it is, and they think it's going to be this touchy-feely, anything-goes sort of place. What they find instead is a high-stress, work-dominated environment. Fortunately, students only receive grades if they're lower than a "C" (otherwise, they need to request them), and juniors have to take a qualifying exam to see if they can "get into" their major. Still, if you want to be around people immersed in the world of ideas—and missing out on the "rah-rah" factor doesn't bother you—Reed is the place. An interesting tidbit is that Reed runs the only undergrad-operated nuclear research facility in the country.

53. **Willamette:** Located in Salem, Oregon, the state capital, Willamette offers a smorgasbord of political internship opportunities. It's a small college with a happy, upbeat energy. While some colleges say they're a "family," Willamette really and truly does value its family-like community. Several professors talked about their students in very protective, caring ways, and one student referred to her Spanish professor as her "Willamette mom." Several of these same professors said there was honestly no other place they'd rather be—not a bad sign, to say the least!

54. **Lewis & Clark:** Another college in the Pacific Northwest, Lewis & Clark is a great place for the environmentally active and socially aware student. Study abroad is big, and one of Lynda's students ended up doing semesters in England, Nicaragua, and Africa. Interestingly, though numbers for acceptance are closer to Willamette's, Lewis & Clark students tend to compare themselves to the Reedies. In walking around campus, you might notice more smokers than at more conservative places, but you'll also hear about more student activism, too. When Eric visited a class, one student announced a "Venezuela conference" that week as well as a Latin American Studies party at his house. Another student responded by saying that a rally was going on that same night. The rest of the students all sort of nodded and jotted down the times.

55. **University of Puget Sound:** At just under 3,000 students, UPS is slightly bigger than some of its Pacific Northwest neighbors, but the campus—with its backdrop of the staggering Mt. Rainier—is quiet and photo-op perfect. The dorms we saw definitely fit the "like palaces" category mentioned in *The Princeton Review*, and the students, in general, seem to be pretty middle-of-the-road politically. They tend to be bright kids who, in high school, might have been seen as some of those kids with "potential" and who are now finding their way.

56. **Eckerd:** Though most of the buildings have the bland, '70's look of a Howard Johnson's, the campus's beauty comes from the ponds, marshes, and nearby river. If you're into ornithology (on our tour, we saw ducks, cranes, and even an osprey) or any aspect of marine biology, Eckerd is worth checking out. Its marine biology building looks like an enormous stealth fighter that just landed on the banks of the nearby river, and it draws a number of students who go on to study not only the marine sciences, but pre-med, too. Eckerd draws a number of regional students who might not have the firepower of some of these more science-oriented kids, but the student body as a whole hails from all over the nation. An interesting program at Eckerd is called ASPEC, or Academy of Senior Professionals. This program, important enough to merit its own building, is comprised of retired professionals from the "real world" who work on campus by getting involved with

classes, attending dinners, and helping with career development. James Michener and Elie Wiesel are two of the more recognizable "professionals" associated with the program. Being in Florida, you might not find some of the vegetarian and vegan options offered at schools out west, but the marine recreation program—free for all students who want to kayak, canoe, or sail—seems to make up for this.

57. **Smith:** Drop your preconceptions about all-women's schools in general and Smith in particular. The women of Smith are sharp, confident, and by no means disconnected from the world. Also, with its celebrity roster of alums, Smith provides any sort of internship or job connection you could imagine.

58. **Macalester College:** Located in upscale St. Paul, MN—but on several streets cluttered with bohemian shops—Macalester offers an intellectual refuge for those who don't mind the cold Minnesota winters. Though the campus buildings themselves might not provide the classic old-school feel of some colleges, there's no denying the scholarly engagement of the students. Macalester is where high-intensity pre-med students mix with laid-back hippies, and genuine diversity rules the day. All the students sing the praises of the excellent quality of the teaching.

59. **Carleton College:** Also located in Minnesota, in the town of Northfield—which, according to one former student, smells of "marshmallows and cookies" as a result of the nearby cereal factory—Carleton should be on the short list of any budding scholar who's also looking at places like Amherst or Middlebury. Carleton shares Northfield with St. Olaf, so young people abound, and you can take the 45-minute bus ride into the nearby Twin Cities, or stay home and bike, cross-country ski, or—more than likely—study. Students tend to be engaged, iconoclastic, offbeat, and fun. In 2006, the residential halls of Carleton began the Dorm Energy Wars to see who could reduce their per capita energy usage most dramatically over the month. These "wars" proved so successful that they've expanded to a number of other colleges. On a less serious note, a student started the "Cooking with Carls" tradition, in which a student, professor, or staff person shares a

favorite family recipe in the student paper, and then food service prepares it for the college!

60. **Rollins College:** Believe it or not, Rollins is the oldest college in Florida. Located outside Orlando in posh Winter Park, Rollins manages to do a good job of getting its students to think globally. It's unusual for a small school to offer majors in Latin American and Caribbean Affairs or minors in African Studies and Jewish Studies, but Rollins manages to do just that. Business is big at Rollins, and you can graduate with an MBA in five years. Rollins is also known for its heavy-duty support system. Its Writing Center, Academic Support Services, and involved professors all make it hard for students to fail.

61. **University of Iowa:** This is one of the state universities that provides education at a bargain price. On top of its big programs in music, health sciences, and the behavioral sciences, the University of Iowa is perhaps best known for its creative writing program and Writer's Workshop. Kurt Vonnegut, John Updike, and Sandra Cisneros are just three of the names who've been associated with the writing department.

62. **Kenyon:** A place for smarties in the Midwest, Kenyon is perfect for the scholarly, well-rounded student who likes the thought of life in small town Ohio. Honestly, we've never met a student who attended who just liked the place—they all *love* it. Kenyon has great programs in English and drama (former students are currently studying both), and its swimming program is one of the best in the country for D-III. Beyond the fact that Bill Watterson, the *Calvin and Hobbes* creator, is a grad, this school is just plain incredible in its own right. It also tends to be on just about every college counselor's "favorite" list, a fact that has made it increasingly difficult to get into.

63. **Grinnell:** This is another hotbed of intellectualism that just happens to be in the Midwest. (Who said bright students had to go "back East" anyway?) Classes are very small, and the students tend to be freethinking, liberal kids who like to strike out on their own. If you're scared of being in the middle of Iowa's cornfields, don't visit, but if you want a place where you'll

truly be challenged, Grinnell is worth considering. The school's Expanding Knowledge Initiative emphasizes the college's focus on inquiry-based, interdisciplinary offerings in its curriculum. New buildings include a student center, four new residence halls, an environmental education center, a gym, and a science center that encourages hands-on learning.

64. **St. Olaf:** Down the street from Carleton, St. Olaf is more of a regional (and Lutheran) presence, but don't let that scare you away. Beyond its nationally-recognized music conservatory, St. Olaf also has some great things going on in other fields, too. Its brand new Science Complex is a sustainable "green" building, and a 1.65 megawatt wind turbine has recently been installed on the campus, providing for a third of the school's energy use. The students are known for their friendly, outgoing nature.

65. **U. of Richmond:** This is one of those "has it all" sorts of schools. Want a pretty campus? U of R's campus is one of the best, with classic-looking buildings surrounding a centrally-located lake. Want a place that's not too big but not too small? Richmond has more than 3,500 undergrads. Want some nature but in a place that's not too rural? The campus is isolated and quiet, but you're five minutes from downtown. Traditionally, Richmond has been a pretty conservative place with a strong Greek element, but that has begun to change. Eric's sister and brother-in-law both went there, and they're independent-minded, globe-trotting, liberal people who loved their experiences. Business is a big major, but all of the other departments provide a challenging workload that ends up surprising some students by just how tough it is. U of R also has a school of Leadership Studies that provides a far-reaching, interdisciplinary look at leadership in all its forms. Big-name speakers from DC are brought in all the time, thanks to Richmond's enormous endowment.

66. **Connecticut College:** When we travel around the country, visiting colleges, we like to ask local college counselors about their favorite, "best-kept secret" colleges. And though Conn. College is no longer a secret, it has been a counselor pick for years now. Connecticut College transitioned from a women's college to coed; there are no Greek societies; and it's known for its strong

professor-student relations. Big programs include the fine and performing arts, environmental studies, and international studies, among others.

67. **Pitzer:** One of the Claremont consortium colleges, Pitzer is the youngest and perhaps most offbeat (in a good way!) of the group. We've sent several students there, and they've loved not only the ability to take classes on all the other campuses, but, just as importantly, what Pitzer is about. Students tend to be socially-minded, and the fact that there's a "social responsibility" requirement further cements the fact that this value is more than just window dressing. Pitzer's study abroad programs also reflect the school's uniqueness, not only in that they all involve home stays, but also because they virtually all happen outside Western Europe. (And those that are set up in Western Europe take place in cities like Parma rather than Rome.) Eric talked to a student on campus, one of the 60% who go abroad, and she told him about the "amazing time" she'd had in Botswana. On a more conventional note, Lynda visited a Shakespeare class one day and was absolutely wowed by the world-class prof and engaged students. Pitzer joins forces with Pomona for athletics to field the ever-intimidating (but actually pretty impressive) Sagehens.

68. **Gettysburg:** Even if you don't care about Civil War history, Gettysburg is good for lots of other reasons, too. Of course, its history department is exceptional, but so are its programs in political science, English, and business. With Washington, DC and New York just a quick train ride away, students are able to pursue internship and study opportunities there, as well.

69. **Occidental:** This is a small, liberal arts college located in a quiet suburban enclave outside Los Angeles. At Oxy, "community-based learning" is more than merely an abstract term being bandied around because they're a nice, liberal arts college. It is, essentially, a program with its own building that supports other departments in finding community connections for their classes. It is also a philosophy that guides much of what the school does academically. Related to this "real world" focus, Oxy has a Department of Diplomacy and World Affairs with a strong UN internship connection. There's also a program called Urban Environmental

Policy, and it, too, seeks to push students not only to make links among the disciplines, but also to push those links into the world beyond.

70. **Bates:** Bates is one of those interesting schools that really and truly does attempt to look at the "whole student," not just his or her numbers. Bates prides itself on its study abroad program—enabled in part by its month-long spring term—and its students tend to be eclectic, original, politically engaged kids. In addition, more than half the courses contain a community service component. Because it's located in Maine, the students tend to be fans of the outdoors (and of cold weather, too).

71. **Lake Forest:** You read right, that's "*Lake* Forest," not "Wake Forest." Though Wake is certainly a good school in its own right, Lake Forest, situated just outside Chicago, makes even more of a point to emphasize strong professor-student relations. The students we've sent to Lake Forest are bright kids who'd just begun to figure out their academic direction. Lake Forest then helped them develop into the successful young men and women we sensed all along they could be. (As cheesy as this might sound, it's true.) Lake Forest has been known as being fairly preppy, but in recent years, it has taken significant steps to improve diversity. Business, economics, psychology, and poli-sci are among the popular majors. An Islamic World Studies program was also recently added. On one visit where a former advisee gave Lynda a personal tour, she visited an upper-level Spanish class that was a perfect example of the high-quality, caring teaching that has long made this college a favorite with us. At lunch time, Lynda and her student had a hard time making choices in the dining hall because there was such an enormous variety of ethnic food offerings along with basic favorites like made-to-order omelettes.

72. **Hobart and William Smith:** Hobart College is for men, and William Smith is for women, so Hobart and William Smith is a perfect blend of single-sex and coed, all at once. The two genders end up doing everything together, but then they have their own home turf to return to if they want. Hobart and William Smith alums tend to be extremely loyal, and as with some of the other schools on this list, professor-student relations are a big deal.

The curriculum involves no distribution requirements. Instead, freshmen take an interdisciplinary class that focuses on how to write and reason better. Interested in marine biology? Check out *The Seneca*, the colleges' own ship. Although Lynda is a landlubber from the desert, she felt not a twinge of sea sickness during her ride because *The Seneca* motors around on the Finger Lakes, which also means it can operate all year round.

73. **Emerson:** If you want to go into broadcasting, journalism, or anything related to media production, this is the place for you. Though a friend of Eric's who attended suggested that Emerson can be a little too pre-professional, she also said it more than prepared her for her work as a producer for CNN. Emerson is great for students with this focus who want something a little smaller (and more liberal) than BU, but who also want the life of Boston. Remember the story about Lynda's advisee who decided to go there to study film? She was ready for the intensity that Emerson provided.

74. **Muhlenberg College:** This Pennsylvania college attracts a student who tends to be pretty focused on his or her future. Premed and prelaw are both big, and so is business. The campus has a more conservative feel, and its Lutheran affiliation contributes to the general lack of slackers. Sports are popular, students are friendly, and Muhlenberg is often referred to as "the caring college." What more could you want?

75. **Washington University:** Located in the middle of the country in St. Louis, Wash U is far from both the state and DC. No matter, it's one of the finest schools around. Lynda still recalls when kids would groan at the suggestion of a college in the Midwest, but that has all changed now. Wash U is *hot* and for good reason. The academics are serious, the programs are varied and flexible, and there's a balance between classes and other aspects of college life. One of Lynda's former advisees, a serious, straight-A kind of girl, loved the fact that she could devote 40 hours a week to dance classes and performances while still keeping up her grades in a rigorous major focused on teaching handicapped children.

76. **U. of San Diego:** USD (not to be confused with the also-great UCSD, in the University of California system) is private and Jesuit. Gleaming white buildings, Southern California landscaping, and its location atop a hill overlooking the spectacular Pacific Ocean might make the campus seem more like a movie set than a university—until you get into classes, that is. Yes, there's a religious component, but it reflects the Jesuit dedication to education. For example, to fulfill the religion requirement, students can take courses in comparative religions or Buddhism. The size fits in that not-too-big and not-too-small niche, too.

Well, that's it for now, but know that we could easily keep going and going. This list, as we said, was meant simply to throw a few names your way and names that maybe you hadn't heard as much about in the normal rush of the day-to-day. Remember that there are MANY more fantastic places worth your looking into. There are Coe and Drew and Bryn Mawr and Austin College and Holy Cross. There are Ithaca and Denison and Lehigh and Rice and Hendrix and George Washington and, of course, McGill in Canada and the University of Edinburgh in Scotland. And then there are Northern Arizona and New Mexico and the whole U of California system. There are too many good places, and every time we, as college counselors, go on a tour, there are always several that make us say, "How is it we know so little about *this* college? Where has it been all this time?" We've been researching and visiting colleges for years, which you need to keep in mind as you look at schools and hear names that maybe your friends don't know about—yet.

Many of these schools won't be for you, but don't worry. As with finding the right match in love, your perfect-fit college is waiting for you out there, somewhere. So look at our list, and then look at other lists. Enjoy the journey of love and life. You have a lot ahead of you.

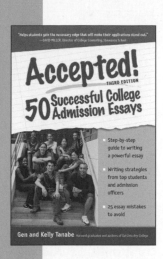

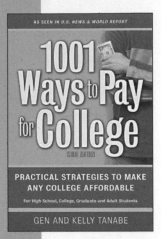

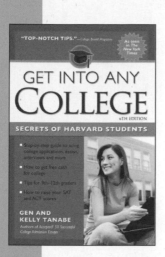

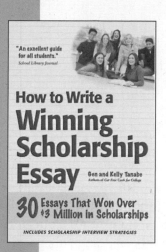

# ABOUT THE AUTHORS

So . . . who *are* these people asking you to take their advice, anyway?

Eric Dawson and Lynda Herring have been college counselors and classroom teachers at Kent Denver School in Englewood, Colorado for most of their careers. Eric earned a B.A. at Guilford College and an M.A. at Miami University in Ohio. He has been doing college counseling for eight years. Lynda earned a B.A. at Stanford University and an M.A. and a teaching certificate at the University of Colorado, Boulder. She has been a college counselor for twenty-two years and was coordinator of Kent Denver's program for nineteen.

Sam Ayers, a former student of theirs, won the 2008 John Locher Memorial Award from the American Association of Editorial Cartoonists, the premier award for the best college cartoonist in the country. He also just won a Truman Scholarship, which isn't all that bad, either.

After having worked closely with students and their families for all that time, Eric and Lynda felt that, despite the wide range of college literature already on bookstore shelves, there was a need for a text that combined concise, no-nonsense information with a light-hearted approach.

Basically, they'd like to return the focus of the college search back to the student—or, in more basic terms, YOU. Along the way, they'd like to remind everyone that there are oodles of great colleges out there and that there are real choices for everyone who wants to attend. (Despite what everyone is hearing in the news these days.)

In short, they'd like to attempt the seemingly impossible: to bring sanity and reason to a subject that, for all sakes and purposes, has gone off the deep end.